16 Clues
to Your Past Lives!

Linda,

Get a Clue!

Love & Light,

Barbara Lane

16 Clues to Your Past Lives!

A Guide to Discovering Who You Were

by
Barbara Lane, Ph.D.

ARE PRESS

ASSOCIATION FOR
RESEARCH AND
ENLIGHTENMENT

A.R.E. Press • Virginia Beach • Virginia

A.R.E. Press
215 67th Street
Virginia Beach, VA 23451-2061

Library of Congress Cataloging-in-Publication Data
Lane, Barbara.
    16 clues to your past lives! : a guide to discovering who you
were / by Barbara Lane.
        p.   cm.
    Includes bibliographical references.
    ISBN 0-87604-421-6
    1. Past life readings. I. Title. II. Title: Sixteen clues to your
past lives.
Bf1045.R43L35   1999
133.9'01'35—dc21   99-10526

Cover design and Illustrations by Steve Ferchaud

Dedication

This book is dedicated to the most fabulous family in the world—my mom Kathleen, siblings Jim, Tahree, and Dan and their families—and my dad John, a past-life philosopher-prince, and my friend Dodie Henson, a metaphysical writer and past-life big sister, both of whom are preparing for their next sojourns to Planet Earth.

Contents

Acknowledgements

With a happy heart, I thank Steve Ferchaud whose brilliant cartoons made me laugh; Joe Dunn, my editor, present-life surfer king, and past-life eskimo; Bob McMillan, past- and present-life fighter pilot, for caring enough to read my work; Brenda English, copy editor, who's trying to keep her head this time around; and especially Stuart Dean, my past- and current-life knight. A heartfelt thank-you to those who were courageous enough to share their past-life clues and stories in this book.

Howard Stern:
Merely every man's fantasy or Howard's past life?

Foreword

Why would a respectable woman with a conservative Midwest religious upbringing be wandering around a sports bar in Virginia asking strangers who Howard Stern might have been in a past life?

Well, a spinoff benefit is that it's a great way to get a date—if we find someone we're interested in, that is. Seriously though, why *was* I spending my Saturday night, December 6, 1997, at *Rampart's* with microphone in hand, asking that particular question?

Of course, I told myself, I'm conducting a "man-on-the-street" (or "woman-in-the-bar") interview to garner a small slice of the public thought on the designated topic. My idea evolved after I was invited to hypnotically regress some of the Stern radio show's staff and affectionate groupies.

Aware of how Howard, Robin, and the on-air staff "ganged up" on their guests, using the element of surprise, I had a momentary flash of them asking me to identify the Undersecretary to the Navy, and how I would have to admit that, although I had been an anchor and reporter for an award-winning, three-hour, morning radio newscast on California's central coast, and although I had worked as a press assistant on Capitol Hill in Washington, D. C., I had no idea.

Even worse, my friends also warned me that I had to be prepared to give my bra size.

So, what is a '90s-kind-of-woman (a.k.a. a former enterprising reporter) to do?

Take back my power, of course! The element of surprise! It was then I got the brainstorm.

I started my interview experiment in a metaphysical bookstore in Old Town Alexandria where I was doing a book signing. Those timid readers ran from my tape recorder like the plague.

Serendipitously, I was to meet friends for drinks at a bar during an Indiana basketball game. Now, this might work, I speculated. After all, these people would have been cheering on their favorite teams and they would have been drinking. This should lower their inhibitions, and perhaps they'd respond to my query even if they thought I was a kook.

I arrived at the bar and waited nervously until the game was over. Now was my chance. I convinced myself to stretch my comfort zone and leave my friends. Reticently I made my first contact. I had forgotten the power that holding a microphone gives—the power to approach strangers and ask them outrageous questions.

I ponied up to the bar and tapped a middle-aged man

on the shoulder. "Excuse me, but if there was such a thing as a past life, who do you think Howard Stern would have been?" I asked in a cracking voice.

Without flinching, he shot back at me, "The first female gynecologist."

Now, I was gaining confidence. I began to approach others who were clustered around the bar.

One young woman blurted out, "Howard was in a harem." Actually I had thought of that one myself, given his seeming obsession with women and sex while wistfully claiming to remain loyal to his wife of many years.

Another yelled out, "A eunuch in a harem."

A third: "He had to have been involved in those Roman orgies." That thought had also come to me since Stern's *shtick* is to shock the senses, hitting morality hard.

The speculation about Howard Stern's past lives was fast, furious, and fun. Two things impressed me about the exercise. The first—that I didn't have to go into a long explanation about what reincarnation is and who believes it. The second—that without knowing anything about clues to past lives, these revelers were able to instantly see a correlation between Howard Stern's public persona and speculate on possible past lives. This reinforced my belief that some of the clues to our own past lives are obvious to ourselves and others. Discovering those clues only requires a shift in perspective. Furthermore, it can be fun. It doesn't require years of elevating our consciousness or sitting in the lotus position.

Not only can we quickly recognize clues to our own possible past lives, but we can pick up clues to our children's, our mate's, or our boss's past lives. Whether we are congregating around the water cooler, going out on a blind date, or sitting in traffic with our car pool, we can enter into a fascinating exploration of our own and others' past lives.

But to finish the Stern story—at Stern's New York radio studio, I conducted a group regression session on five of his staff members and regulars. All five quickly went into a relaxed hypnotic state, and when they were asked, they began to tell me their past life recall. Since each account was so captivating, all five subjects were going to accompany me on air and would return to the same relaxed, hypnotic state when I put my hand on their shoulders.

Once on the air I fortunately didn't have time to think about myself since I had to focus on my five subjects. And Howard. And Robin in the control booth. And the paraphernalia on the walls. In fact, I was so concerned about Howard not being brutal to my subjects (although I knew they were used to his style) that I forgot about the possibility of being embarrassed.

Steve Grillo was first. Under hypnosis, he recalled being a nineteen-year-old stablehand named Christopher, who lived in a small, rural town in the northeastern United States in the 1800s. He described his house as having a mud floor. As Christopher, he felt that other townspeople were jealous when he was rewarded with a better job. After Stern mentioned my Civil War book, Steve recalled not wanting to fight in that war, although he was against slavery. Steve, who has stomach problems in this life, recalled dying from a stomach infection.

We got into trouble over Crackhead Bob. Because Howard knew I was having difficulty understanding Bob's mumbling, he jumped in as regression facilitator and ultimately asked Bob if he had been Confederate General Robert E. Lee. Bob replied, "Yes."

I had to backpedal, and I said that perhaps Crackhead Bob had been among General Lee's troops or had heard of him. This was a good case for demonstrating that the therapist should not ask leading questions.

Nicole Bass, World's Largest Female Wrestler, remembered living a utopian lifestyle in an advanced society in what may have been the British Isles in ancient times. Nicole, now in a deep state of hypnosis, recalled a society in which there was no concept of aging.

Doug Goodstein appeared to be a credible source. He summoned up memories of being a Jew in Poland during the Nazi invasion in 1939. He remembered the Nazis dragging him into the streets, knocking him unconscious with a rifle butt, and leaving him for dead. The sensation of the gun's blow was so real that Doug, as Nathan Stelensky, had to grab onto his chair to counter the resulting spinning sensation. Sadly, he recalled losing his sister Jenny in the riot. He also found that, although he returned home, he was never quite the same physically or mentally after the impact.

Fred, the Elephant Boy, saw himself as a successful merchant, Clement Lewistine, who owned a large mercantile store in a town outside of Chicago. He was happily married and died of tuberculosis.

The subjects were wonderful, Howard was amazingly kind, and the show flowed quickly to a conclusion. Afterwards, all five subjects admitted that although they heard the on-air jokes, none of them felt like laughing— an indication of their deep state of hypnosis.

Although Howard claimed he was afraid to find out who he was in a past life, I couldn't help but wonder if any of the suggestions from my woman-in-the-bar interviews had been right. After all, these respondents had observed clues about Howard Stern's public character that could be indicators of one or more past lives.

If people who listen to the Howard Stern show can speculate on Stern's past lives, think how easy it will be for you to look for clues that may point to your own past lifetimes as well as those of your family, friends, and co-workers. Consider then, these sixteen clues, as a kind of looking glass that will reflect back some of your own possible past lives and a glimpse into your very soul.

Introduction

While looking for past-life clues in your present life and putting the puzzle pieces together, you will find the endeavor to be a fascinating journey in self-discovery. By considering the concept of reincarnation and examining how these clues manifest in your life, you can become aware that you are a multidimensional being as you unearth some of your past lives.

In addition to looking at your life in this new light, you can use these clues to get insights into the people and the relationships that are important to you. You will also find great conversation questions to ask your co-workers on your next lunch hour. Or you might find a way to enhance your understanding of your next date.

The search can be an adventure into awakening. As you become more aware of your past lives, you may be able to see your life as part of a bigger picture. The wisdom you acquire can help you to grow, expand, and even rewrite your past.

As you become more aware of these new possibilities, you will be able to make healthy choices by getting rid of old, unproductive patterns that you may have repeated for centuries. Through this simple technique, you can not only create and enjoy more quality in your life, but you also may get a glimpse of your immortal soul and realize that death is a transition during which you reconnect with loved ones, rejuvenate your spirit, reevaluate your life, and prepare for your next assignment!

The "Table of Contents" is a ready reference to the sixteen past-life clues which you will be unearthing. Each chapter is designed to focus on a specific clue. The personal examples in each chapter will trigger some of your own clues—whether consciously or subconsciously. As I accumulated those stories, they triggered my own past-life clues, some of which might not have occurred to me otherwise.

At the conclusion of each chapter is a series of *Thought Stimulators*. The questions are designed to prompt your thinking about your possible clues. I urge you to thoughtfully answer all of the questions you can and write down your responses. This exercise will help to give form and substance to your past-life puzzle pieces. It will also give you a benchmark as to where you are in the process at any given moment. Be peaceful and know that the information will unfold naturally as part of your evolutionary process.

Do not concern yourself if no clues appear to you in some of the chapters. Even a few clues may be enough to give you the framework for a past life, the details of which will evolve over time. Additional answers to the questions may come little by little—in a few days, a week, a month, or a year. Review the Thought Stimulators occasionally to examine your latest insights.

Also keep in mind that we gravitate toward different lifetimes at different periods in this life. You can review these questions periodically to see if you are beginning to direct your attention to another time period.

The last chapter—chapter Seventeen—shows you how to position the puzzle pieces that you have collected throughout the book so that you can interpret them and solve your own past-life puzzle. This chapter also explains how to connect your past life with that of someone who is significant in your current life.

Observing and recognizing the clues in your life is an ongoing process. We all are works in progress. As you search to know and understand yourself through your past, you will live your present more fully and create the future of your choosing.

So fasten your seatbelt to travel into the sacred time of the soul. Enjoy the trip and the resulting soul growth!

John Wayne:
Were his cowboy roles good acting—or remembering?

Clue 1

❂

Interest in a Certain
Historical Time Period

While many of us recall history classes that plagued us with memorizing soon-to-be-forgotten facts that we believed held no relevance in our lives, other students found such classes to be alive and meaningful. Their imaginations brought forward personalities, situations, and time periods, normally relegated to history books, into a kind of personal reality. Often, certain time periods were more real than others to these students.

Little did Shelby Morgan know that, as a youngster, she had already embarked on a search for her soul's history. She read every book she could find about World War II and the German military and showed no interest in the American forces.

Determined to go to Europe, at fifteen she traveled to the Chicago shipyards to seek work on an ocean-going steamship, but she went to the wrong place to apply for a job. Undaunted, she later saw an Air Force recruiter whose visit to her home was cut short when her father told her that she could join that service as long as she didn't have to put on a uniform.

While working a night job to pay her way through Memphis State University, out of the blue she saw a newspaper ad for an interview with Trans World Airways (TWA). She was selected out of a sea of young, hopeful faces. Germany was the first country she visited as a TWA employee. She knew she had come home. "Germany was me," she said.

Back at her home base in Kansas City, she gravitated to German and Jewish friends. When flying, Shelby was in her element. She loved airplanes and took flying lessons. "It was so easy, I was one with the airplane," she recalled. Her instructor would always comment on how well she landed the plane. Eventually, she became the flying school's first female instructor.

Shelby had always believed that she had been in the German military in World War II. She began praying and meditating to get a confirmation of her belief. Thirty months later she had a vivid dream.

In the dream, she saw herself as a German soldier sitting on a knoll looking down on infantry, tanks, and trucks. The soldier was waiting for an airplane to pick him up. He was between thirty and thirty-five years old, brown eyes, blond hair, and a pleasant look. Although he did not like war, he took pride in himself and his responsibility, liking a job well done. He was wearing brown spit-shined boots that came to just below the knee. Shelby could smell the matching brown leather strap across his shoulder connecting to his waist.

Then the plane landed, the soldier boarded, and the vision ended. Shelby's prayers and the resulting revelation have given her the verification that her present life in many ways has been a continuation of her previous European incarnation.

When Daniel Bierman first went to San Antonio, Texas, he was disappointed to find that the Alamo was downtown. Internally, he knew it was supposed to be out of town. Immediately, he felt a strong personal attachment to the battle at the Alamo.

Later in life, through a psychic reading, Daniel was told that he was one of the children in the Alamo. That helped to explain his special affinity for the site, because he felt no attachment to other historic battlefields. While visiting the Alamo, Daniel experienced a feeling of protection and pride. He felt he had a firsthand understanding of why the Texans were willing to defend the Alamo against Santa Anna's forces.

History books reported that Daniel's past-life persona— Enrique Esparza, the oldest child in his family— was twelve years old. The psychic had indicated that Daniel was only about nine but large for his age. Synchronistically, a guide at the Alamo told Daniel on a 1985 visit that a bible had been found a month earlier, indicating that Enrique was born September 5, 1828, making him eight at the time of the battle.

Later a psychic counselor told Daniel (Enrique) that he, the psychic, had been one of Enrique's younger brothers and that Brian, who worked with Daniel, was the other younger brother, Manuel. After his past-life discovery, Brian mentioned that he had unconsciously referred to people of Mexican descent as Manuel when he didn't know their names.

About a year after this revelation, a female friend of Daniel's was told that she had been Enrique's sister.

Enrique, who was spared when he hid in the hay, saw the Alamo's dead burning in two pyres. He is credited with giving a firsthand report of the battle from the Texas side.

What do you have in common with Shelby and Daniel? Perhaps more than you may think. Although you may not hurry out to buy a vintage airplane or antique rifle, you may have your own proclivity for a specific historical time. Although the time period(s) that interest you may not affect many areas of your life or be as intense as Shelby's, you should begin to pay attention. Even if your interest is as subtle as a breeze, you should heed it. Such interest can be an indicator of a past life.

Each of the Civil War and medieval reenactors who I regressed to past lives for my earlier books—*Echoes from the Battlefield* and *Echoes from Medieval Halls*—all remembered past lives in the times they are drawn to reenact. But this concept—a past-life connection with certain time periods of interest—is even more widespread.

On a recent plane trip from Britain to the States, my seatmate told me that England has a large contingent of reenactors—The Sealed Knot—of the British Civil War. Some of the reenactors believe they may have been reincarnated from that era. I also heard at a conference about the Rainbow Family, which includes thousands of people around the world who believe that they may have been Native Americans in a past life.

Although the numbers of Revolutionary War reenactors have dropped since the Bicentennial, around 5,000 troops reenacted the Battle of Yorktown in the early 1980s.

Katharine Bradley, who grew up near Valley Forge, Pennsylvania, spent her weekends at age five re-creating actions of the Revolutionary War with her family. They could be found in colonial dress in a log cabin farmhouse where George Washington was once headquartered. While her mother cooked period dishes and her sisters used drop spindles to spin raw wool into yarn, Katharine would draw on a slate board.

While part of a Viking encampment group participating in the Military Through the Ages (MTA) competition in Jamestown, Virginia, in March 1996, I saw living historians (historical re-creators) who recreated the campaigns of Caesar, Napoleon, Boudicca, Kaiser Wilmhelm, and U.S. Grant, and there were Vietnam War reenactors as well.

There are reenactors who recreate the Indian wars, Rendezvous reenactors who portray French traders and Native Americans, and others who are frontiersmen and mountainmen.

Besides reenactors, there are the curators of historic homes and employees and volunteers at sites such as Willamsburg, Virginia, who dress in period clothing. There are also round tables, collectors, and Internet groups that are interested in specific historical periods.

Many who are drawn to the past participate in activities from more than a single historic era. Since each of us has had more than one past life, it's not surprising that once the reenactors' souls become linked with history, they expand their interest into more than a single period. Chances are good that you, too, are interested in more than one time period. In fact, it is probable that we are interested in particular periods at certain points in our lives when we are working out lessons with one or more of the same people who were incarnated with us in those particular times.

With this in mind, let's begin to give some attention to this first clue to one or more of your past lives. Answer all of the Thought Stimulators. Use these questions as triggers to evoke thoughtful answers.

Remember, additional answers to the questions may

come over time, so review the Thought Stimulators occasionally to examine your latest insights.

Also, since we gravitate toward different lifetimes at different times, review these questions periodically as you begin to direct your attention to other time periods.

Now that you have begun to focus on one or more historical time periods, keep this in mind as you begin to seek other clues to your past lives!

THOUGHT STIMULATORS

• Do you have a fascination for a certain era or eras in history? Perhaps the medieval or Renaissance era? World War I or the Wild West? Why?

• What history class did you like best? Why?

• Are you a member of a historical group or round table or would you be interested in joining one?

• Do you search historical Internet sites or are you in any historical news groups?

• Are there any periods you particularly dislike? Why?

• When did you first become interested in each period? What triggered the interest?

• Do your family, friends, or mate share the same interest? Or not?

• Have you been interested in different historical time periods at different times in your life?

• What of significance happened at those time?

• Who was (were) the significant person (people) in that life?

Shirley MacLaine:
Dancing her way up Machu Picchu (again).:

Clue 2

✿

Fascination with a Geographical Area or Setting

Have you ever stopped to consider that you may be the only one in your family who has a yearning to visit Goosebay, Labrador? A gaucho ranch in Argentina? To cross the Death Valley desert? Go on a mountainous trek in Nepal? Hike through a rain forest or jungle?

Did you grow up on a farm but crave the glittering lights of the big city? Live in a high-rise building but hunger for the wide open spaces? Always feel the urge to live by the water? Has an area other than the one(s) you have lived in felt strangely familiar? Have you always disliked cold weather? Have you wanted to keep returning to a specific vacation spot?

If you are already aware of preferences for certain areas, settings, or climates, so much the better. If not, let your subconscious mind simmer and let the following anecdotes trigger memories of your own favorite places.

While doing radio interviews on reincarnation throughout the United States, Canada, and South Africa, I enjoyed asking the on-air staff to look at clues that could point to their own past lives.

WXCD Chicago radio personality Kevin Matthews said he loves Ireland. He also enjoys the outdoor life, including fishing and hunting. It is entirely possible that Kevin led one or more rugged lifetimes in Ireland and the British Isles. These proclivities also may have originated in a lifetime as a pioneer or mountainman.

Morning radio co-hosts Pam Bunch and Christian Myers of Central Pennsylvania's WBHV may have known each other in a past life. Every time Pam visits the New England area—particularly New Bedford—she has déja vu (feeling as though she had experienced this before). She's also had feelings of familiarity while visiting Walden Pond. Pam has read *Moby Dick* and seen the movie and has a strong interest in whaling vessels of the 1800s. Christian is interested in sailing, grew up in New England, spending his free time on boats. Were these co-anchors working together with a different kind of anchor in their past?

Pat Benton of WOOZ radio in Carterville, Illinois, said he is captivated by the Old West, the time of King Arthur, and the ancient Greeks. On-air partner Ryan Patrick says he wouldn't mind returning to what he feels were the simpler times of the 1920s, '30s, and '40s, as well as going back to ancient Rome.

In addition to media personalities, many of my clients, conferees, subjects, and friends have expressed an affinity for a particular area or setting.

Since he could remember, Art, a successful Ohio businessman, has had a need to go to Scotland, and he's always wanted a kilt. (Now, his son wants all the males in his wedding party to wear kilts.) Art regularly wore a tam-o'-shanter in high school. A high school tennis player, Art recognized the tennis strokes as being the same as sword strokes. Later, while in the army, he developed a passion for pugile-stick fighting which duplicates a single-stick type of fighting in Scotland.

When Art first visited Scotland, he toured Rosslyn Chapel outside Edinburgh. At a particular spot in the chapel, Art felt pulled toward a wall as if he sensed an entrance there. Simultaneously, he felt the weight of monk's robes. The guide explained there had once been an opening at the exact spot Art had identified and that monks had entered there. Strangely, Art had always felt he had lived as a monk in a past life. Art also intuitively knew that there had been a book of stone in the crypt below the chapel which was only for the eyes of those who had undergone a special initiation, something the guide later verified.

Since his pilgrimage, Art has visited the crypt many times in meditations and has seen portions of these initiation rites. In contemplation, he has envisioned himself in a past life lying prostrate on the crypt floor and having a sword placed on his chest. He said that this was a recreation of the crucifixion, with the sword simulating the cross. The arms of the initiate simultaneously embraced the sword, which represented knighthood, and the cross, symbolizing Jesus. Art believes the initiation symbolized the acceptance of Jesus and the commitment of a Templar Knight at the same time. (The Knights Templar was a religious military order established at the time of the Crusades against the Muslims.)

In this lifetime, Art has had problems accepting Jesus. He has joked about religious wars—especially the Crusades which involved the Templars, and in which, Art said, "We kill for Christ."

As a teen, Art was a member of de Molay, an organization for the sons of Freemasons. (The counterpart for young women is Rainbow Girls.) De Molay was named after Jacques de Molay, the last grand master of the Templars, who was summoned by the pope to answer charges against the order and was later burned to death. As a de Molay, Art ushered at functions for the Knights Templar, now another branch of the Masonic organization.

Having a passion for the highlands and particularly the older, rounded mountains, Art was in heaven in Scotland. Art said the wind, a constant in Scotland, has blown life into him and brought a smile to his face. For him, walking the hills of heather and looking out at nearby islands was like going home.

The American West has always lured thirty-eight-year-old bartender Roseanne Nablan. She spends her vacations on Native American reservations. During a regression, she saw herself as Running Deer, a Native American woman dressed in soft deerskin and moccasins, fishing in the Mississippi River. She was twenty-two at the time of her death. She was hit in the back of the neck with an axe-like tool. Her murderer was an Indian man from another tribe. Roseanne recalled the painful wound while she lay dying for two days but looked forward to going to the Great Spirit.

My client Lidija recounted to me that in 1992, while she toured the Gettysburg battleground alone, she broke down and cried. Six years later, on a steamy September morning in Alexandria, Virginia, Lidija recalled a past life as the wife of a Southern officer. They had lived happily in Virginia. Her husband had been involved in the devastation suffered by men on both sides of the Gettysburg battle 135 years before. After her regression session, Lidija told me that she envisions herself living happily in the South in the future.

In addition to her fascination with the South, Lidija has had a long-standing enchantment with Egypt. She found herself making a series of trips to Alexandria, Egypt, to visit her then-Egyptian boyfriend, who was well-to-do. She loved being treated as royalty—having a limousine at her disposal and being wined and dined. A royal Egyptian past life? Quite possibly.

A living historian of medieval times, Ann has always been captivated by the British Isles. The thirty-six-year-old journalist was so enamored of that area that she traveled extensively in England and Scotland. Her interest also prompted her to begin work on a novel that included a Scottish personality.

During one long hypnosis session, Ann recalled three lifetimes in the British Isles. In the first, she was a six-year-old English girl whose mother was the housekeeper of a manor house. Ann began her regression in the second life as a Scottish boy whose mother was a cook. The boy eventually learned to fix wheels for a trade, married, fathered five children, and was killed when struck by a wagon. Ann consistently spoke with a Scottish brogue throughout her recall of the second lifetime, but she had no accent during her third recalled life. That life was in Scotland in 1563 and involved a married woman named Ann whose sister was involved in a love triangle with Ann's husband.

After reading this chapter you may never think the same way about planning your next vacation. Perhaps it will take on meaning as a pilgrimage to a possible past life. As you reflect on past trips or enjoy new ones, you

can begin to monitor your feelings and pay more attention to people and events that may have seemed at one
time to be happenstance.

So, too, with the environments in which you live. Begin to notice how you feel when you are in a given location. Remember that there may be fewer accidents than
you might suspect in life. Look for connections.

Sometimes we can only see our clues by a retrospec-
tive look at what has happened in our lives. Clues can
seem to be slow in coming, and we can be even slower in
piecing them together. As you read on, you will begin to
observe how many of the clues in the stories told here
are intertwined and how they collectively create interesting snapshots of past lives.

In addition to beginning to look at your life from a
fresh perspective and responding to the Thought Stimulators at the end of each chapter, let's enlist your subconscious to assist in alerting your conscious mind to
meaningful information or patterns that you can begin
to piece together. The best time to program the subconscious mind is just before sleep. Pay attention to any
messages you receive, particularly as you awake, in moments of quiet reflection, while driving, or while performing any rote activity such as brushing your teeth.

THOUGHT STIMULATORS

• Have you been drawn to a special geographical area, climate or setting, wanting to travel or live there? The British Isles? Egypt? The mountains? The ocean? Do your ancestors live in this area?

• Have you felt particularly comfortable or uncomfortable in the places where you have lived or when visiting your favorite place or places?

• Have you had déja vu in any of these locations? Did something there seem familiar? Did you know your way around better than you should have?

• Look at what may appear to have been coincidences, significant people, or events that took place in any of these areas.

• Have you lived in many locations or been relatively sedentary?

• Do you gravitate to settings unlike where you live?

• Do certain cultures, ethnic groups, or ethnic foods attract you?

• Did learning a second language come easily for you?

• Have you wanted to keep returning to (or avoiding) a specific vacation spot? Does something unusual happen each time you return to a similar place?

Camelot

JFK and Jackie:
Perhaps comparisons to Camelot were no coincidence.

CLUE 3

✤

Art, Artifacts, Music,
Dance that Resonate

Do certain paintings, sculptures, art works, or artifacts haunt you? Does a certain piece, style, or era
of music tug at your heart strings? Do you prefer big
band music to symphonic strains? Have you always enjoyed American Indian chants, African drumbeats, Latin
dancing or ballet? Does folk or country western dancing
appeal to you more than ballroom dancing?

The art, music, and dance that you enjoy may assist
you in unfolding more pieces of your own past-life
puzzle. In fact, it can be more helpful than you might
suspect because the arts use intuition, feeling, and the
subconscious instead of simply drawing on intellect and
the conscious mind.

Take Marge for example. The striking-looking performer called me immediately after she returned from visiting the U.S. Holocaust Memorial Museum in Washington, D. C. I detected a note of urgency as she asked if I could fit her in for a regression session.

When she arrived at my Alexandria office, Marge told me that when she saw a picture of three American GIs standing next to a Jeep after having freed Jews from a concentration camp, she burst into tears.

A past-life regression session revealed that Marge had been an American soldier in France. Both the soldier and his troop were captured and beaten by Nazis. The Americans died next to a Jeep, thwarted from being able to come to the aid of the Holocaust victims.

After the session, Marge recounted how her father, an American GI, had met her German mother in Europe. Marge had been born in Germany and spent several years on military posts in that country. She felt comfortable while on the base, but less comfortable with the Germans. Still, she didn't want to move to the United States. Unfinished business?

The regression session, triggered by the photo at the museum, shed a new ray of understanding on Marge's twentieth-century life, her feelings about Germany, and her relationship with her parents.

I visited the Prado Museum in Madrid with my friend Barry. I was amazed to find a painting of a medieval Spanish woman who resembled a woman I had just met in Virginia. In the next hall, Barry found a painting of a medieval Spanish man who resembled a man he had known in Virginia. Interestingly enough, the two medieval Spaniards depicted in the paintings were married.

Since Barry and I had recognized these two related Spaniards from the past, perhaps we had also had a medieval Spanish incarnation in which we had known them. This scenario reinforces the point that author Gina Cerminara said psychic Edgar Cayce made, that "an interest in things Spanish argues a Spanish incarnation ... and that it may serve to lead to people with whom we had previous connections in the same lifetime."[1]

Another case that demonstrates Cayce's belief that "any impelling interest very probably streams from activity in a previous lifetime" is Dave Purschwitz's hunt for a particular type of artifact. At the age of twenty-six, he bought his first Minié balls for twenty-five cents each. Those inexpensive but genuine Civil War-era bullets sparked Dave's initial interest in the Civil War—an interest that has now spanned thirty years as a Civil War reenactor. It became an expensive hobby that has permeated nearly every area of his life.

After six years as a Civil War reenactor, Dave heard about his great-grandfather's involvement in the Civil War. Twenty-six years after buying those Miniés, a past-life regression enabled Dave to relive his own amazing Civil War past as his own great-grandfather.

Like art and artifacts, music can trigger an interest in a particular past life or be a sign of one.

Guy Rathbun has hosted *The Club McKenzie*, a radio show in San Luis Obispo, California, specializing in jazz of the 1920s and 1930s, for more than twenty years. At times, he has dressed in period clothing while on air. Perhaps a past life as a manager for talent in the roaring '20s?

Felicia instinctively knew how thirteenth-, fourteenth-, and fifteenth-century music had been sung. In college, she found that her alto voice was perfect to perform the medieval and Renaissance music. Before college she sang in her high school madrigal club. She first was drawn to Renaissance music as a seventh grader and taught herself the recorder. Today, she performs on the recorder at the Maryland Renaissance Festival and for medieval reenactors at the Society for Creative Anachronism (SCA).

Under hypnosis, the forty-two-year-old recalled an Elizabethan life as the mistress of an Italian manor. As Bianca, she ran the household while her husband Frederico was interested in education and the arts, including playing the flute.

Sandy Arnold has been in a belly dancing group for twelve years. A writer and researcher from Harrisburg, Pennsylvania, she believes that there is a special bond among the group's eight members. The dance troupe has no leader and is named "Kismet" because the women feel that destiny has drawn them together. Most of the group have elaborate costumes which cost well over $1,000. Six of the eight women have traveled to Egypt since they joined the troupe.

By now, you should be thinking about what forms of art, artifacts, music, and dance strike a chord with you on an emotional level. In the *Saturday Night Live* skit, Coffee Talk, the host says, "Talk amongst yourselves." So, take charge. Discuss this topic with others. Ask others how they would assess you in these areas. The Coffee Talk hostess also chats about getting *verclempt*— teary-eyed. So, what art touches you enough to make you *verclempt?* If you say nothing touches you in such a way, you have been working entirely too hard lately. Reevaluate your life.

If you believe football is the only art form that moves you (to the couch), this is your chance to redeem yourself, impress your significant other—or maybe find one—and make yourself a more "well-rounded" (culturally-speaking) individual.

THOUGHT STIMULATORS

• With which pieces, styles, types, and periods of art or artists do you resonate?

• What pieces, styles, or eras of music or musicians move you?

• What styles, cultures, or degree of formality of dance do you find compelling?

• Do you collect artifacts from certain periods?

• Why do you suppose you like these particular styles?

• Does your family like the same styles or different ones?

• Have you been attracted to different types of art or music at different periods of your life?

• Why do you think you changed your taste at those times?

• What else changed in your life around the times your taste changed? Did any people move out of or into your life before or during those times?

Cher:
Past-life fashion queen?

Clue 4

✪

Your Taste in Fashion, Jewelry, and Home Decor

A quick examination of the contents of your closet can tell someone a lot about you. More interesting than what someone sees on the surface is the possibility that clues to your past lives may be hanging in plain view. The clothes and accessories you wear can be a telltale past-life sign. You may, in truth, be wearing your past lives on your sleeves.

If we glanced into Paul Jones's closet, we'd find fifteen different historical uniforms, with all their components. The thirty-eight-year-old Alexandria man owns Revolutionary War, Civil War, and World War II attire. His Civil War uniforms alone range from early and late Civil War impressions to his generic, special and dress uniforms, duty uniforms, winter coats, and accouterments for a variety of Civil War reenacting scenarios.

Randy Bennett, a fifty-year-old salesman, has unconsciously used period clothing to decipher and refine elements of his conscious awareness about his past lives. He obtained his first Civil War uniform while a history major in college. Next, he purchased a World War I uniform. Unaware of the hobby of reenacting, Randy wore his initial purchases while deer hunting alone.

Since that time, he has reenacted the Civil War as a private and a captain, a Confederate and Yankee, in the artillery and infantry. While reenacting the Civil War, he met several men who he instantly recognized.

Randy's great-grandfather, who served as a Confederate, was imprisoned after being shot in the foot. The Marines refused Randy partly because of foot problems. His ancestor was five-feet-seven-inches tall with brown hair and blue eyes. Randy is five-seven with brown hair and blue eyes. Randy's signature is nearly identical to that of his Civil War ancestor.

As for his World War I uniform, he has gone through a few in order to get the correct past-life one. Trying various uniforms out, Randy pays attention to which ones feel comfortable. While doing impressions of World War II, he was bothered by reenacting as an American or British soldier. He did, however, enjoy acting as a World War II Russian and was told he looked the part. Still, the hammer-and-sickle insignia on the uniform's right breast bothered him. Eventually he realized that he must have been a World War I White Russian loyal to the czar. Now, he's the only man in his unit to have a czarist tunic and a rifle with the czar's crest on it.

Randy once made himself a miner's outfit and used a pie pan to simulate panning for gold. It was not an unfamiliar feeling for him. Another time he transformed himself into a Viking, making everything from a shield to shoes.

He also purchased a complete kit to portray a U.S. infantryman in the Indian Wars (1850s-1883). He is one-fourth Cherokee. Although he had made everything "from rope to soap" and had spent more than $1,000 on the uniform and accouterments, he didn't feel right in that role and couldn't wear the uniform.

His feelings were reinforced by his vivid dream about the Indian Wars. In the dream, he recalled himself as a sixteen-year-old, wearing a blue coat and sky blue pants and riding a horse. After being stabbed in the stomach and falling to his knees, he saw leggings approach and felt the pain of being scalped. From his dress, Randy thinks he had been a young federal cavalryman or more probably a *federale,* (a Mexican soldier) who wore surplus U.S. Army uniforms that had been sold to the Mexican government after the American Civil War. (Leggings were worn by the Apaches in the Southwest.)

A look in Randy's and Paul's past-life closets should relieve any guilt about accumulating clothing. Who knows? Perhaps it's past-life therapy at its best.

My past-life closet is bland next to Randy's and Paul's. In my closet hangs a blouse I bought several years ago. The blouse has Egyptian motifs on it. Even though I haven't worn it lately, I can't bear to get rid of it since it is covered with hieroglyphics, reminding me of my Egyptian lifetimes.

I also have noticed that a large picture of three Egyptian female musicians or muses, purchased at the Cairo Museum and hanging above my computer, is identical to one of the designs on the blouse. Of course there's my cartouche, not to mention the ankh ring and various Egyptian-style earrings and necklaces. I'm embarrassed to admit owning a gaudy green top plastered with a gold profile of Nefertiti, two ankhs, and the title, African Queen.

All of these items complement the bust of King Tut, the framed picture of the boy king's throne, the pyramid and obelisk, and other signs of Egyptian life in my living room, bedroom, and hallway.

My decor hasn't always had an Egyptian flavor. When I was married and lived in California, I described the decor as early cowboy and Indian. The wallpaper, bedspreads, artifacts, pictures, and stoneware had a decidedly Native American influence. The couches had the appearance of rawhide and the furniture was heavy, dark, and chunky—a modern version of a primitive look. It fit in well with the redwood walls and the casual lifestyle. The home happened to be near a Chumash Indian site. My former husband wore cowboy boots and jeans, and I loved to run barefoot or wear the closest thing to moccasins. I also wore Indian-patterned clothing and jewelry and listened to music with Indian undertones.

The day I filed for divorce was the day I planned my trip to Egypt. Later, when I returned from that pilgrimage, I hung my Egyptian paintings, displayed the objects d'art, and added touches that included large baskets filled with tall papyrus reeds.

Since moving to Virginia and becoming involved with Civil War reenactors and, later, medieval reenactors, I have acquired two lines of what I believe are authentic reproduction clothes. I have taken pains to research and select fabrics, colors, patterns, trim, styles, and accessories that were worn in each respective era.

On the first occasion that I dressed in my Civil War outfit, I felt extremely youthful and perky. I was astonished since I should have been exhausted due to sleep deprivation. This feeling matched those of several other Civil War reenactors, who told me that they felt younger in their uniforms. If these men had been soldiers in the

Civil War, it would make sense because most reenactors are older than the soldiers they portray.

I commissioned my outfits since I do not sew. My first seamstress was in North Carolina. She asked me if I wanted her to make a modern party dress with the watermark silk material left over from my bright red Civil War day dress. After giving it some thought, I decided to design a ball gown top so that the huge hoop skirt of my day dress could double as a ball gown. Much to my surprise, a helpful civilian reenactor found in a historic costuming book a red Civil War dress that was designed to double as a day dress and a ball gown.

As for my medieval garb, the clothing I designed was historically accurate for thirteenth-to fourteenth-century France. During the course of my research, I had became fascinated with the Cathars. They were a religious sect, largely based in Southern France, who believed in reincarnation and who were persecuted for heresy in the thirteenth century. I made a point to make a spiritual journey to Carcassone and other Cathar sites.

Mary Church is fascinated by the Revolutionary War era and has a collection of 3,000 books on the topic. It's no surprise that Mary has decorated her Maryland house with fixtures, furnishings, and placements befitting a middle-class eighteenth-century lifestyle. Mary, an interior designer, has plain Shaker-style furniture, wooden floors, and swags and festoons for window treatments. She can easily imagine herself living comfortably in a frontier town, is familiar with the customs of the time, and can bake bread and cook over a hearth.

As a child, she was obsessed with Willamsburg, Virginia, and would beg her parents to take her there. When they arrived, she would run around the town, feeling completely at home.

Because of her love for Williamsburg, she majored in

interior design and minored in anthropology so that she
would be able to research the architecture in that recon-
structed town. Later she owned Canterbury Interiors in
Washington, D. C., and she would periodically go to
Williamsburg to relax.

As an interior designer, she concurs with my theory
that different people gravitate to different time periods.
Mary says, "Our lives mirror our environment." She also
points out, "The time periods of the furniture speak for
themselves, matching the person with the color and
style." She believes people have a comfort zone that in-
corporates definite time periods, wallpaper, fabrics,
color, and style. She calls it an unconscious choice.

She described several clients with tastes in different
styles. A stark, utilitarian environment with Shaker-style
furniture; a fourteenth-century Marco Polo look with
heavy tapestries and antiques;, and the Victorian period
with dark colors, massive furniture, and papered ceilings.

I wondered how a couple who had two distinct and
different styles coped? She said usually each one would
have a room with their preferred style to which they
could retreat. But, she cautioned, if there was no agree-
ment on a period, the couple sometimes split up.

Do we need to factor interior-design taste and past-
life decor into a relationship equation? Interesting
thought. While our subconscious environmental comfort is important, so is the comfort of the clothing
that expresses who we are.

Most of my Civil War and medieval reenactors say they
are more comfortable in their respective costumes than
in their twentieth-century attire.

It's not only comfort, however but also sometimes dis-
comfort that gives us a past-life clue. Nick, a medieval
reenactor felt instantly part of medieval times from the
first moment he dressed in tights and a blousey shirt.

Even though the thirty-nine-year-old resides in Virginia, he did not feel the same comfort when he wore a Civil War uniform.

As proof, he showed me two photos of himself—one looking stiff and uncomfortable in the Civil War attire and one in which he appeared smiling and relaxed in medieval clothes. One explanation could be the memories that the uniform subconsciously triggered for Nick who may have fought, been wounded, been imprisoned or died in that war.

Some reenactors get married in their garb. Many display evidence of their historic hobbies in their homes. One Civil War reenactor's home I visited looked like a Civil War museum. Besides a vast collection of books and artifacts, he had actually sewn Civil War flags and uniforms and constructed period furniture.

THOUGHT STIMULATORS

• Do you have a distinctive style of dress? The prairie look? The cowboy look? The sporty look? The intellectual look?

• Do you find you repeatedly buy one or a few particular types of clothes?

• In which clothing and accessory style(s) do you feel most comfortable?

• What clothing styles do you wear most? Do you wear a lot of one color?

• Do you find yourself buying clothes and jewelry with cultural or historical motifs?

• Do you have a tattoo that is an indication of a particular era?

• Do you notice a consciously planned or unconscious historical theme in your home decor? What architecture do you like?

• Do you notice your clothing, home decor, or architectural styles changing at different times in your life or while relating to different people? (Perhaps you are working out specific lifetimes with them.)

• Do you ever portray historical characters, people from specific eras, or ethnic groups at Halloween? When you were a child? Why did you think you made those choices? Who would you choose to be now?

• Do you recall any particular generational fads that could point to a historical time period for a larger group of people; e.g., toga parties during the 1960s college days?

Ted Turner:
Was his *Gettysburg* role a walk-on or a walk "back"—in time:

Clue 5

✣

Movies and Books
that Resonate

Whether we are inveterate movie watchers or not, some movies make a bigger impact on us than others. We already know what general categories of movies we like. Although we may not consciously dissect the film, we also know our own criteria for a good movie. In your case is it: Your favorite actor? An adventure? A tear jerker? A catharsis? The ability to make you temporarily forget about your own problems? Your relating to themes which play out in peoples' lives? What else keeps you riveted to your seat, feeling as if you are living each scene with the actors?

A movie could be meaningful to you because you have been in a similar situation, area, or relationship sometime in your past—whether in this life or a distant one. You could have lived in that time period. A movie could trigger a remembrance of a past life or a past-life issue through the costuming or the set design. An actor, accent, or phrase could touch a chord in you. Perhaps the movie hits on a theme that has special significance to you now or in the past, or more likely in both cases.

It is no surprise that the vast majority of Civil War reenactors respond to the movies *Gettysburg* and *Glory*. Many of them were in the real-life battles those movies portrayed. Even television mogul Ted Turner couldn't resist getting into the act. For the movie, Turner joined one of the Confederate units that made Pickett's Charge.

A historian for the movie *Glory*, Brian Pohanka was exhilarated during the filming of the night attack on Fort Wagner. He described how he and thousands of reenactors were swept up in a realistically created sense of danger when they charged across the moat.

An eerie feeling overcame Dave, another reenactor, when he was being crammed into a cattle car with other prisoners for the television movie *Andersonville: The Diary of Josiah Day*. The experience, similar to the one of arriving at Andersonville that he recalled during a past-life regression, aroused his emotions.

While it seems obvious that Civil War reenactors would be passionate about Civil war movies, I was not prepared for how such movies affected me. Having never been interested in war films, I was dumbfounded to realize that I was spellbound by *Glory* and particularly *Gettysburg*. I was shaken by the fact that the officers—former school chums and best friends—were destined to fight each other. *Gettysburg* was the final catalyst that brought me into the Civil War era and found me regressing reenactors, writing a book, getting my own nineteenth-century dresses, and speculating about my own Civil War past life.

Many medievalists also have repeatedly watched the movies *Brave Heart* and *Rob Roy.*

If reenactors are imitating their own past lives, what about the correlation of actors and their roles? Oscar-winning actor Michael Douglas said that his life paralleled his role in the thriller *The Game.* He played a billionaire investment banker, who was a second-generation success like himself; Michael followed in his father Kirk's Hollywood footsteps.[1]

Could pop icon Madonna, who did a remarkable transformation into Eva Peron, wife of Argentinean leader Juan Peron, actually have acted her own past life in the movie *Evita?*

The two women's lives certainly had parallels—both grew up in lower income families in small towns. Both believed they would become powerful. Both moved to large cities with little money and were known for using their wiles and shrewdness to move up the career ladder. Maria Eva Duarte was a popular radio and film actress. Madonna is one of the world's top-paid entertainers. Both have made a big impact on the world. Eva inaugurated welfare programs for children, workers, and the underprivileged. Madonna's impact is an artistic one, although as she continues to recreate herself, her legacy may expand as Eva's did. Evita died in 1952. Madonna was born in 1958.

My friend Jim Quayle has spent years finding connections between movie stars and their pasts. Sometimes, Jim believes, artists are replaying their previous lives.

Marlon Brando is remembered for his role in Francis Ford Coppola's 1971 hit, *The Godfather.* He played an aging Mafia Don with a large, violent, unruly family. His son-in-law was unfaithful, mistreated the godfather's daughter, and was eventually killed by the gangster's son, who became the next godfather.

Brando himself is the head of a large family with numerous children from several marriages and relationships. About two decades after the release of the *Godfather*, Brando's son Christian was accused of killing his sister's lover. Part of his defense was that she had been mistreated.

Jim believes he has traced Brando's identity back to a Spaniard, Rodrigo Borgia, who became Pope Alexander VI. Even in his prominent position as head of the Catholic Church, Borgia had a large family of illegitimate children from a number of mistresses. One son, Cesare, had his younger sister Lucretia as his closest female friend. During his father's papal reign, Cesare quarreled with his sister's husband and had him murdered.

Historical movies such as *Saving Private Ryan* and *Shindler's List* not only could help activate past- and present-life memories, but also could serve a larger function—to help heal the collective consciousness. By mobilizing mass consciousness to better understand a major world event and to help resolve it, playwrights, movie directors and actresses may be serving to elevate the world view and facilitating healing en masse.

The same criteria and concepts hold true with the books and even magazines we choose to read.

In junior high school, when the bookmobile came around, Susan was drawn to take out books on Native Americans. Years before she had saved the cards from cereal boxes that had information and pictures of Hopi Indians who wore loin clothes before the presence of the white man. As an adult, Susan saw herself in a regression as a Hopi man who was haunted by visions of a coming massacre. He kept this secret in his heart until his prediction became a reality. Feeling the shame of survival because he was spared, the old man willed his own death.

Through a series of synchronistic experiences that guided her, Susan has lived and worked with the Hopis, been given two ceremonial pipes, and attended a Native American sweat. She continues her quest for spiritual growth and her mission, a mission that may be inextricably linked with the current Hopi nation and which harkens her back to her past life.

Susan also thinks it's entirely possible that the soldiers and cowboys who slaughtered the Native Americans in the past have returned as some of the Native Americans who dress like cowboys and are now troubled with alcohol and depression.

My favorite novel is *The Mists of Avalon* by Marion Zimmer Bradley, an Arthurian tale that was told though the eyes of a woman. Serendipitously, more than ten years ago, friends congregated aboard a yacht to discuss our possible medieval past lives. Imagine our surprise when the boat drifted toward Avalon, an island off the California coast.

THOUGHT STIMULATORS

• Have you watched a particular historical movie or movies more than once? Could you imagine yourself in that time period?

• Do you find that you read books about a certain time period, place, or hobby? Do they elicit a strong emotion in you? Identify that emotion.

• To which character(s) do you relate? Why?

• What are your favorite movies for costuming and set design?

• Do you perceive a situation or relationship in your current life that is similar to one in your favorite books or movies?

• Do you observe any patterns from the books or movies that are repeated in your life now?

• Have you been interested in different types of books and movies at different times of your life?

• What perspective do you take on the film or book? Which side are you on? Why?

Jay Leno:
He was funny even as a kid. When did he practice?

Clue 6

❂

Vocations,
Avocations, Education

Let your imagination project you into the future. What if school vocational counselors directed students into college programs and careers based partially on the talents and skills the students had acquired in past lives? Could you envision a human resources department making job recommendations using past-life knowledge as one criteria for hiring? Too far-fetched? Perhaps, but handwriting analysis is being used in European firms as one hiring tool for selecting prospective candidates, and the practice has spread to some American counterparts.

In the immediate future the only place we'll probably see past-life career counseling on a large scale is on *The X Files*. This isn't to say, however, that such counseling hasn't been or isn't being suggested by a small number of psychologists, regression practitioners, astrologers, and psychics.

Known for his thousands of life readings, American psychic Edgar Cayce counseled youngsters and adults to develop along certain career paths which would enhance skills acquired in other lives.

In a reading for a six-month-old boy, Cayce viewed a prior French life in which the subject had worked with disease, and he predicted that as the child matured, he would show interest in a medical career. As Cayce foretold, as a child the boy had a phobia about germs. By the time the boy was ten, he was delivering papers to save money for medical school.[1]

If Edgar Cayce had been alive to give Jay Leno's mother vocational counseling for Jay when he was still a baby, Cayce might have said, "Encourage that kid to be funny. He was funny before and he'll be funny again."

Jay's mother, not recognizing his humor as a marketable skill, told her son that there was a time to be serious and a time to be funny. When they took a trip to Disneyland, Jay asked, "Can I be funny now?" She replied, "Not now."

Now the host of the *Tonight Show* is known as the hardest working man in show business, but he has worked hard at it for a long time. Leno got his first laughs when he was four and asked innocently, "How come girls have humps like camels?" From then on, he never did anything unless someone was watching. In fourth grade he told his teacher, "Robin Hood couldn't boil Tuck because he was a friar."[2] The rest is history.

Little did Mary know that an obsession she had felt as a child would later turn into a business. Growing up in a small town in Maryland, Mary had always wanted to be a Native American. When the neighborhood kids played "cowboys and Indians," she always chose the Indian role.

They built a shelter and used sticks for horses. Her play was so real to her, she described it "as if you were there." She also had vivid dreams of being a Native American who died of starvation.

In junior high school, she built an entire Algonquin village, complete with bark-covered dome-shaped huts. She created and wore an outfit that would have been worn by a young Native American who had lived along the Ottawa River in Canada. Although she didn't do much research and relied heavily on intuition, she later verified some of the information that she had only sensed.

Several years ago Mary had a pet store that sold feed and tack. She also included Western wear and custom-made costumes for Rendezvous reenactors—those who reenact as French traders and Native Americans and who highlight the customs, speech, and tools of the period. She sold such goods as authentic moccasins and hides decorated by Native Americans. As a student, she was already preparing to work with her future clients.

I regressed Rob Gibson, thirty-eight, from Rochester, New York, at Gettysburg in July 1998. Rob's avocation was Civil War-era photography, including tintypes and ambrotypes. Imagine our surprise when, under hypnosis, he recalled himself as a young drummer boy in the Civil War. When the young drummer and a friend had photographs taken in Baltimore to send back home, the boy was captivated by the process. Later in the war, he became a photographic assistant who developed battle maps. In a final, dramatic scene, he recalled helping take photos of those accused of conspiring in the assassination of Abraham Lincoln as they were being hanged.

After the regression, Rob told me that he had picked up drumming at an early age, even though the rest of his family "couldn't play a shoehorn." He also said that as a youngster he was fascinated with Civil War photography, poured over Civil War photographs, and was a perfectionist about Civil War uniforms and dressing up. He recalled getting chills when he accidentally stumbled onto Ford's Theater in Washington, D.C., where President Lincoln was shot.

Since the regression, Rob has purchased a Civil War-era camera lens, once owned by a Baltimore photographer who took pictures for the Confederacy. I reminded him that in his regression, the drummer boy had his photo taken in Baltimore. Rob also has been invited to do photography at the White House and to visit Matthew Brady's old gallery on Pennsylvania Avenue. Could the Washington office where he was an assistant have been that of the famed Civil War photographer Brady?

Although some Civil War lives have been painful, Rob's nearly three-hour regression session was filled with so much visual detail and learning that he became nostalgic when he returned to the twentieth century. These remembrances contributed to a major life change for Rob. The weekend Rob had his Civil War regression, he decided to turn his avocation into a vocation. If you visit Gettysburg, look him up and get a genuine Civil War-era ambrotype taken by a real Civil War photographer.

While Rob Gibson had no trouble bringing forward his photographic skills, Edgar Cayce noticed that sometimes former talents are forgotten and need reawakening. Without use they could atrophy, while with practice, such skills may lead to abilities in the next life.

Psychologist Edith Fiore, Ph.D., has helped patients reawaken abilities by facilitating their return to previous lifetimes to find the source of talents, skills, and interests.[3]

One of my colleagues regressed a client to a lifetime in which she was an artist. My colleague suggested that under hypnosis that the client would bring forward artistic abilities. Prior to the regression, she had shown no interest in art. After the regression, she bought an easel and paints, took a sculpting class, and created some remarkable paintings.

Keeping this in mind, start to examine the more obvious aspects of your life before moving on to what may appear more subtle. Take a look at your career path or various career paths. By looking at each job from a number of perspectives, you can observe what influenced you to make these choices and whether you were using your talents.

Next, focus on your continuing education. Look at trade schools, additional degrees, or even classes you have taken just for fun. Fly fishing or yoga? Interior decorating or karate?

Also explore your avocations and hobbies and the passion behind them. How did these interests begin and how would you like to see them evolve?

Finally, look at your abilities. Are some so natural that you hardly recognize them? Have you gotten the opportunity to use these abilities?

Investigating these areas may not only give you a fresh perspective on your talents, career, and education choices, but also may point you in the direction of one or more of your past lives. Remember that you may subconsciously gravitate to degrees, training programs, and careers that have come from your soul's past-life interests.

THOUGHT STIMULATORS

- What do you particularly like about your career?

- What other careers have you had? How did you feel about them? What patterns do you see in them?

- What influenced you to go into this (these) field(s)? Do you feel this (these) career(s) suited you?

- If you could have chosen another career or may choose one in the future, what would that be?

- What job-related skills have come easily?

- What classes did you particularly enjoy? Which classes came easily?

- Why did you select your field of study? What or who inspired you to make your academic selections? If you could go back to school, what would you study?

- What activities do you perform strictly for pleasure and in which do you excel? What avocations and hobbies do you enjoy?

- Do you do calligraphy or another activity from a different era? How did these interests begin and how would you like to see them evolve?

- What activity are you so passionate about that you not only would do it for free but also would spend your own time and money? Why are you so passionate about it?

.

**Shirley Temple: If it takes 35 lives to become
a child prodigy, she must be on life 35.**

Clue 7

✧

Knowledge or Talent
Beyond Experience

How do we explain child prodigies, the children who, as tiny tots, can sit down at a piano and write music or do some equally magnificent task that most of humankind, even as adults, cannot achieve?

Some people might explain these children through the concept of genetic memory—the passing down of information and abilities through the genes. This theory could apply to children whose parents or even ancestors had the same abilities that these youngsters possess.

But what about the case of Georg Frederick Handel? The boy was born in Germany in 1689 to a non-musical family. Not only that, the boy's father, a barber-physician, discouraged his son from playing music.[1] If his immediate family was any indication of his ancestors' lack of musical ability, Handel's case could discount the genetic memory theory. In any case, reincarnation was Edgar Cayce's explanation for child prodigies like Handel. He placed talent and interest firmly in the heredity of the soul rather than in the heredity of the genes.[2]

Young Shirley Temple captured the hearts of her audiences. At the age of three, she began acting and taking dance. Serendipitously, a music teacher tipped off Shirley's mother, as the mother was about to take Shirley home from dance class, that studio talent scouts were on their way to the dance studio. Although 200 other girls and boys were prepared and well groomed, the movie people were captivated by Shirley. Six days later, Shirley had a screen test.

As a child, she could act, sing, dance, and hold her own with the major celebrities of the day. Dancing became reflexive and natural; she could pick up tap steps by hearing the beat and mimicking other dancers. In addition to her talents, Shirley exuded a charisma and star quality that has not been equalled by any other child star and rarely equalled by an adult. Had Shirley been influenced before birth by her mother who, while pregnant, had consciously played classical music, read good literature out loud, bathed herself in color and aesthetics, and gone to local movies? Or had Shirley chosen a mother who would set the conditions in place for Shirley to pick up her performance career where she had left it in a prior life?[3]

Chances are high that if psychic diagnostician Edgar Cayce had been given the opportunity, he would have found more than one lifetime in which Shirley had been a performer. Cayce might have discovered that she had danced, sung, and acted many times; while in the trance state, Cayce indicated that about thirty-five lifetimes were required to attain the expertise of a master such as Handel or Beethoven.[4]

There are others whose talents are so developed at such a young age that these abilities may have come from a past life. As a youngster, Patty Duke won an Oscar for her role as Helen Keller. Another natural is child star Macaulay Culkin, who acted in *Home Alone*. And child entertainer Michael Jackson. Musical genius Stevie Wonder. Chess player Bobby Fischer. Golf pro Tiger Woods, who golfed as a tot. The young Australian pianist David Helfgott whose troubled life was the basis for the movie *Shine*.

If we accept Cayce's theory, chances are good that: Tony Robbins and Wayne Dyer had other speaking gigs on Planet Earth, perhaps dressed in white tunics; Shakespeare (whoever he was) put quill to paper or papyrus in an earlier time; Babe Ruth (a pitcher as well as famed hitter) had tossed the discus; Mohammed Ali was a gladiator; generals Colin Powell and Herbert Norman Schwartzkopf rubbed shoulders with Alexander the Great; Martin Luther King motivated the masses before the 1960s civil rights movement; and John F. Kennedy might have been a pharaoh.

For those of us who haven't reached the stature of a superstar, Cayce's estimate of thirty-five lifetimes for perfecting our talents to genius level can be an inspiration.

First, we can release the notion that these superstars appear to have just made it, even if it looked easy this time around. Chances are that they've had plenty of struggle and discouragement in past lives. Even after many lifetimes, fame isn't usually immediate or effortless. Wayne Dyer will testify how he bought up all his first books, stored them in his garage, and hit the small-town lecture circuit, radio, and bookstores—in this lifetime.

Second, we can have a fresh appreciation of our own abilities and refrain from comparing ourselves with others. For the first time, we can imagine that perhaps we are a "nine" (out of thirty-five) at public speaking and a "three" at sports. Being the best we can be and living up to our potential can coincide with being at peace with our gifts.

Even though we may not be considered genius level, there may be information or skills which come easily to us and for which we have no explanation.

Author Taylor Caldwell wrote detailed medical information in one of her novels without any research. Caldwell was later regressed by author Jess Stern and was found to have unearthed the medical information and details in other books from her past lives.

My friend Marilyn's story is inspirational. Marilyn Frost had been a home economics teacher who decided to become a professional photographer. Without taking a class, she began taking outstanding photographs. Within months, one of her flower images was selected out of 25,000 prints for a calendar and other photographs found their way onto greetings cards.

Marilyn discovered that in a prior life she had been a model for French impressionist painter Pierre Auguste Renoir. Marilyn told me this information while we were driving up the California coast to Monterrey. When we pulled into our hotel, we were astounded to find the lobby filled with Renoirs, which we took as confirmation of Marilyn's story. I have no doubt that Marilyn's gift was developed over many lifetimes.

As a child, Susan "healed" her friends by giving them kool-aid™ mixtures. She was also awed by doctors. Recently the forty-seven year-old dietitian from Pennsylvania was led to buy the book *Medicine Women*. She had an emotional response to the story of one of Germany's first female physicians, Dorothea Erxleben. Because she was a pioneer for woman in her field, Erxleben's graduation had to be approved by the king in 1754. Susan suspects that Erxleben's life in the eighteenth century could have been one of her past lives. As a woman, the German doctor had cause to fight the patriarchal system; Susan has had her own challenges within the political framework of her profession. The good news is that Dr. Erxleben won her battle!

Three-year-old Kiersten baffled her family with stories of her past life. She talked of a sister who died in a house fire and said she didn't know where her sister had gone. Kiersten said this was from her "other born" (life) when she had her "other face." For several months, she told the rest of her family, "My sister is coming to live at our house." Three months later, Kiersten's mother found out she was pregnant.

Kiersten continued to surprise her family with information she had no way of knowing, even recognizing people she had known before. She told a physician friend of the family that she and the doctor had painted little pictures of faces that people sent to faraway friends. The doctor was shocked; no one there knew that his hobby was painting miniature portraits.

Carlos Ruiz' story is intriguing. The Venezuelan had long been puzzled by information he intuitively knew. His family and friends did not share his desire or talent, but Carlos learned English on his own in sixth grade. He acquired twenty language records and, in three months, was speaking English better than a friend who had taken specialized classes.

In 1981 Carlos had a vivid dream that a man who called himself Woodrow Wilson appeared to him. Carlos looked up the name in an American dictionary. To his surprise, he found that Woodrow Wilson was the name of the twenty-eighth president of the United States. He was shocked that the small picture in the dictionary was identical to the man in his dream. He enlarged the picture, and it has hung in his office ever since.

During these past seventeen years Carlos has been plagued by a variety of unexplained parallels, knowings, and serendipitous events. As a baby, he was a silent observer—not unlike Wilson. Although unusual for boys, Carlos took typing and shorthand in high school. Mr. Wilson studied both when he was sixteen.

As an adult, Carlos stumbled into a career in international relations and received a master's degree from an American university abroad. His company sent him to Carlisle, England. Carlos later discovered that Carlisle was Mr. Wilson's favorite vacation spot.

On a trip to Washington, D.C., Carlos went to the National Cathedral where he burst into tears at President Wilson's tomb. The White House, when he visited it, felt strangely familiar.

Carlos also felt comfortable in Wilson's Washington, D.C., home. He was attracted to a portrait on the stairway, which the guide said was Wilson's most beloved picture. While looking at a portrait of Mr. Wilson's first wife and three daughters, Carlos had to fight back tears. He also knew that a baseball in the home was signed by King George V—not the usual baseball autograph.

The list of Carlos' unexplained knowledge in regard to Woodrow Wilson goes on. In September 1998, Carlos came to my Virginia office to find answers to some gnawing questions and to have a series of regressions. During the sessions, he uncovered information—details, names, places—about Woodrow Wilson that he says he had not known before. For example, under hypnosis Carlos saw Americans dressed in period attire, an old kitchen with an iron stove, and received the name Tommy—all of which were unfamiliar to a Latin American, but consistent with America in Wilson's time. In another past-life scene, Carlos saw Wilson in a railroad station waiting for someone coming from Ohio and proceeding to Amsterdam. Later, Carlos found an Amsterdam, Ohio, near Columbus. Moving forward in his regression, Carlos' past-life personality looked into the mirror and saw Mr. Wilson and his shiny patent shoes and felt the soft texture of his hat.

Could this Venezuelan man, obsessed with an American president who is relatively unknown in South America, have been Mr. Wilson? A close friend of the president? A political colleague? These are possible explanations.

A third-cousin of Edgar Cayce, Warren Cayce Underwood began to cry uncontrollably the first time his mother took him to Gettysburg. After returning from the trip, the teen joined a reenacting unit. A short time later he came to me for a regression. His mother and I sat in amazement as he described being involved in combat at a place that we identified as Fredericksburg. His mother informed me that he had never been to Fredericksburg nor had he read about the battle. What also surprised Warren's mother was his change in speech pattern, intonation, and vocabulary, none of which she had heard before. Gale Cayce claims that she ordinarily can't break her son's habit of "talking like a typical teenager."

J. C. Clayton, a.k.a. Spider E. Veins, is the producer and host of the NABC radio show *Fuzz Box* which is heard throughout Southern New England and Arizona. In May 1998 he told me incidents that tie into what he believes may have been a past life. At an early age, he noticed that he had an unlearned talent: the ability to read palms. He claims to have had the drive even as a baby to become an artist. As a child, he was compelled to write stories.

J. C. was drawn to history, particularly nineteenth-century France, and he was preoccupied with horror, vampires, and Edgar Allan Poe.

J. C. not only relates to the work of French poet Charles Baudelaire and the poet's fascination with the macabre, but he also suspects that he may have literally walked in the poet's shoes. At nineteen, J. C. first became aware of Baudelaire. What shocked J. C. was that the poetry he had written when he was twelve was amazingly similar to Baudelaire's writing and content. When he read Baudelaire's work, he had an eerie feeling as if he had written the words himself.

Baudelaire is considered one of the revolutionary nineteenth-century European poets and achieved international renown as a symbolic poet. During his lifetime he had a somewhat melancholy temperament. J. C. says he "personifies melancholy," and like the French poet, spent his adolescence being isolated and depressed. Baudelaire was a spendthrift and squandered most of his inheritance; J. C. has no concept of saving money.

Besides his poetry, Baudelaire was a literary and art critic and spent several years translating and analyzing Edgar Allan Poe's works.

Could J. C. Clayton's inclinations be right about having been the French poet? Quite possibly. Both had a fixation on the macabre. There is also J. C.'s compelling interest in nineteenth-century France.

But the strongest evidence may be his unlearned abilities. How did Clayton know how to read palms? It is possible that, given Baudelaire's interest in the supernatural, he would have had a working knowledge of palmistry. An even stronger possible connection was Clayton's compulsion to be an artist and his uncanny ability to write stories as a child.

Take a look at your life. Have you ever just "known"

something? Has a skill come exceptionally easily for you? Perhaps this, then, is another clue which will give you more puzzle pieces to your past.

THOUGHT STIMULATORS

• Does an ability or talent seem to come naturally to you, i.e., a sport, a musical ability, a grasp of mathematics?

• Is such a talent or ability so natural that you hardly consider it an ability?

• Are you surprised that others can't demonstrate such an ability as easily as you?

• Do other members of your family or friends have the same or similar abilities or talents?

• Can you recall any natural abilities you demonstrated as a youngster?

• Have you instinctively known information?

• What was the topic of such information?

• When did you start to observe such information?

• Have you received any outside verification of the information that you intuitively received? Have you received any additional information?

Steven Spielberg: His movie directing began in childhood; perhaps the theater was his life in another time

Clue 8

❃

Childhood

When we were kids, some of us turned old tables into lemonade stands. While growing up, Ryan Patrick used such a table to set up and run his own version of Jerry Lewis' telethon for muscular dystrophy. Ryan said he had a fascination with the telephone and had always been a ham. His telethon entertained him for hours at a time.

As early as he could remember, Ryan also created his own shows. Today, he is a radio personality on Carterville, Illinois, station WOOZ-FM and thinks of himself as a "natural" on the air. Ryan says that he is a good character actor and has a passion for doing comedic theater. His reading list includes stories about his favorite comedians—George Burns, Jack Benny, and the Three Stooges.

Some children would think of dressing for their school's career day as a doctor, lawyer, or some other equally traditional career. Not Pete McMurray. When he was five years old, he came to career day dressed as singer Tom Jones. Pete's voice can be heard nights, from seven to eleven, on WCKG in Chicago, Illinois. He claims that he's always been obsessed with Hollywood stars, primarily the Rat Pack. He waits eagerly for each new *People* magazine and reads it cover to cover. In his dreams, he has the sensation that he knows Bruce Springsteen personally.

These on-air personalities are no different than many of the megastars and celebrities who wanted to be in entertainment from an early age.

Howard Stern always knew that he wanted to be on radio. As a skinny, young kid, he envisioned having his own show and making a major impact on the radio industry. Jim Carrey knew as a child that he would become an actor. So did Tom Hanks, who told his high school acting teacher he was going to make it. Kathy Kinney in the *Drew Carey Show* knew, too. As youngsters, Steven Spielberg was directing plays and filming movies; Bill Gates knew he would be a huge success as a computer whiz; and Ross Perot was developing his entrepreneurial skills—delivering newspapers by horse to save for a car. Brook Shields began her acting career as a baby model. Cybil Shephard was a teen model. Tracey Ullman said that, as a youngster, she used to visualize accepting an Emmy.

The fact that Norma Jean was born in a charity ward and later placed in a children's home could have inspired her to create a fantasy life. At seven, she had her own piano and music lifted her spirits. One of her favorite pastimes was to go to the Saturday movies. As a teen, she would act out the adolescent roles she saw, and she adored following the latest hairstyles and fashion. She was later to become one of America's leading sex symbols, Marilyn Monroe.[1]

At the age of nine, Elvis got his first guitar. He learned to sing by listening to records and the radio and from singing in church. Elvis said that the first thing he remembered was sitting on his mama's lap in church when he was two. "All I wanted to do was run down the aisle and go sing with the choir. I knew it then, I had to sing." That's where Elvis said that he learned to move his body. "When I started singing, I just did what came natural . . . "[2]

While her single parent mom worked as a nurse, Whoopi Goldberg's real school began in their sixth-floor apartment when she turned on the television. She entertained herself with a world of pretend and thought of herself as a fantasy character. Her friends were the actors. As Whoopi grew older, she was involved in an after-school community theater for kids. To her, it was like being in a candy store. One day she could be Eleanor of Aquitaine; the next she could fly like Peter Pan. She could pretend to be a princess, a teapot, or a rabbit.

Whoopi took her mother's advice: "You can do anything you want when you act." The high school dropout transformed herself into a household name when she turned her passion for show business into a reality.[3]

The daughter of a brick layer and an Olympic medal winner, Grace Kelly grew up in a family that was active in competitive sports. She, however, enjoyed ballet and developed what would become a lifelong passion for dance, through which she first saw herself as a performer. As a child, she made up games and stories with her dolls; as a teen, she excelled at acting, developing a fervor for expressing deep feelings on the stage. While still a preteen, Grace was captivated by the audiences' approval and the glamour of acting. Little did she know that she would attract world acclaim and a glamorous lifestyle befitting a movie star and real-life princess.[4]

Gracie Allen went downtown practically every day after school and strolled from theater to theater. Determined to get into show business, she would gaze at the pictures in the lobby, dreaming of the day when her picture would be posted. When she was six, her older sister called her up on the stage to entertain an audience by doing an Irish jig.[5]

The son of a Soviet officer, young Mikhail Baryshnikov fantasized about performing. Although his father disapproved of the theatrical atmosphere, the boy remained interested. He initially wanted to become a concert pianist, but when he was exposed to ballet at twelve, he took an immediate liking to it. His acceptance at the Riga dance school was Baryshnikov's springboard to becoming one of the world's most famous dancers.[6]

During his childhood, Johann Sebastian Bach wanted his own copy of a manuscript volume of a clavier composition so badly that he spent many moonlit nights copying it in secret. His brother had not wanted him to know about the "forbidden music" and took Johann's finished copy away. Johann's futile efforts weakened his eyes but illustrated his early passionate drive for musical composition.[7]

Did these childhood dreams keep these luminaries persevering until they made it? Was it the past-life training that inspired these children's dreams?

The childhood play activities of Ryan, Elvis, Whoopi and Pat could be indicative of their past lives. Ian Stevenson, M.D., past-life researcher at the University of Virginia, found that children who recall past lives often play at their former occupation. One story from his collection was that of a young boy who had formerly "been" an auto mechanic. The child spent hours under his family's couch pretending to fix cars. Another youngster, a teacher in a former life, would imagine being a teacher. A third child, a shopkeeper in a former life, opened a make-believe biscuit shop.[8]

Todd has had a deep love affair with Native Americans. His mother, Mary, says her son was obsessed with that culture at the age of four. Soon he began to read books about Native American history and crafts. Still four, he asked if he could be a Native American when he grew up. He was devastated when his mother explained to him that his ancestry lay elsewhere.

He loved the outdoors and by age seven would go into the woods to camp alone at night. Sitting at the campfire, Todd would become enmeshed in the experience as he listened to taped Native American chants. Concerned for his safety from wild animals, Mary would drive out and observe her son from a distance. But Todd was content, unaware that he was experiencing his Native American past life for which he always seemed to yearn.

Now thirty, Todd is an artist in the Native American style. Without formal training, his skills range from painting to beadwork, from tanning hides to decorating skulls, and from making arrowheads to playing a Native American flute.

A self-taught authority on the culture, his decor includes peace pipes, drums, and jewelry he has made. From the age of ten to fifteen, he relished dressing in Native American attire—even wearing a feather in his blond hair. During that time, he made and wore fringed leggings and a shirt made of leather.

From childhood through his teenage years, Allen Patterson enjoyed books and movies about Colonial America, the Revolutionary War, and the Civil War.

Patterson, a former Air Force pilot and chaplain, developed a great interest in freedom and independence. In a past-life regression conducted by hypnotherapist Henry Bolduc, Allen recalled being a signer of the Declaration of Independence. In another regression session, the seventy-three-year-old who resides in California saw himself as a brunette woman whose fiance was a Confederate soldier, killed in battle.

Such early interest in past lives isn't unusual. While I found that eight of twelve of the Civil War reenactors in my study were "hooked" as kids, history teacher-reenactor John Robinson believes more than ninety percent of reenactors acquired their interest as pre-teens. This is similar to Stevenson's finding that past-life memories begin to fade before the age of ten.

The nervous system is not fully formed until the age of about six. Regression therapist Dr. Bruce Goldberg says that for the first few years of children's lives, their skulls have small openings which may allow the soul or subconscious mind to escape and communicate directly with the child, allowing them to bring their past-life memories into conscious awareness.[9]

For these reasons, I paid attention to the reenactors' childhood years. I found that many Civil War reenactors played Rebs and Yanks as children while some medieval reenactors pretended to fence with tomato sticks or to joust. Some of these childhood games were a recreation of their past-life death scenes. This corresponds with the children Stevenson found who played as soldiers and remembered dying as soldiers.[10]

While my past-life information came from adults under hypnosis, Stevenson discovered most of his cases in areas of the world like India and Asia where the majority of the people believe in reincarnation.

To me, it was logical that while more reincarnation

cases would be reported in a culture conducive to this philosophy, cases of childhood past-life recall also must occur in the West. Western parents may more easily dismiss, even discourage their children's memories because the parents do not have a cultural context from which to support this belief. Until recently, most American parents probably have not listened to their children when it comes to past lives. If a child talked about a past life, parents would pass it off as make believe.

On *The Oprah Winfrey Show* on March 1, 1994, American parents admitted just that. Carol Bowman, the parent of two children who recalled former lives, urged parents to listen to their children's accounts with an open mind. In her book, *Children's Past Lives*, she advises parents to listen calmly to the child's account and note whether the child's tone is matter-of-fact, whether they recall the memory consistently, whether the information is something they couldn't have known prior to recalling the past life, and whether there are present-day corresponding behaviors or traits.[11]

An increasingly supportive philosophical climate and increased media exposure are now making it acceptable for some children to speak out and be heard. I encourage every adult to be an enthusiastic and supportive ear to children. In dealings with children, listen to any clues they might give to describe a possible past life. Ask follow-up questions. Help facilitate their understanding of their journey, which may evolve piecemeal. And, I think, we should be just as enthusiastic and supportive in reviewing our own childhood clues and helping to piece them together for our own understanding of ourselves.

THOUGHT STIMULATORS

• Recall the costumes (Halloween or otherwise) you selected (or would have liked) as a child.

• Would you have changed costumes at different times in your life? When? Why?

• What costumes would you select now? Why?

• Are there certain people from this life with whom you could see yourself in connection to a specific time period?

• Are there other people who you would feel more appropriate with in another particular era?

• If you were an actor or actress, what costumes and roles could you see yourself playing?

• Did you repeatedly pretend to have a certain occupation in play?

• As a child did you recall a former lifetime or glimpses of one?

• Did you have a fascination for a certain time period as a child?

• Did you repeatedly play at dying a certain way?

• What names did you call your dolls or animals? What nicknames did you give to others or did you pick for yourself?

• Did you have an "imaginary" playmate? What was their name? What do you remember about your playmate?

**Princess Di: Perhaps royal intrigue and neglect
had been her companions more than once**

Clue 9

❁

Recurring Patterns

The whole world watched as the melodrama of the personal lives of Princess Diana and Prince Charles unfolded. Much of the planet's populace was fixated on the couple from the moment of Lady Diana's courtship by Britain's heir to the throne right through the dream-like wedding.

Diana was a fairy-tale princess when she stepped from the glass coach at St. Paul's Cathedral. But the royal carriage which transported the couple after the marriage ceremony may have been less a symbol from *Cinderella* than a subtle reminder of the couple's other royal marriages in other times.

The wedding was just the beginning of the drama. The

people were to find out years later that the shy young woman, who had always wanted to marry a prince, had had fears and misgivings even as she walked down the aisle wondering where her rival for the prince's attention, Camilla Parker Bowles, was seated.

Perhaps those of us who have been commoners have wondered for centuries: Was being a princess all it was cracked up to be? For all of our supposed sophistication, we had again fallen under the spell of the princess myth when Princess Di came along. We saw the outer appearances—jetsetting, hobnobbing with celebrities, wining and dining. Eventually, however, Princess Di began to tell the world what we've suspected all along—that castles can be cold, titles can be hollow, and royal marriages can be painful. A saddened Di began to divulge a behind-the-scenes tale of political intrigue, an aloof royal family, and a marriage of betrayal. She told of depression. She told of feeling like a prisoner in her castle life. She told of the prince's friends who advised that she be put away.[1] She told of starving herself—her habitual bulimic coping mechanism. She told of her own eventual extramarital romance in an attempt to find love.

This story just as easily could have been told in the Middle Ages. We could envision it coming from a lonely princess dressed in a purple velvet houppelande (a floor-length garment with large, hanging sleeves) and wearing a cone-shaped hat. Her romance could have been with her liege man.

Prince Charles' story was equally disheartening. He had been forced to marry for political reasons. The one he truly loved was not of royal lineage. Perhaps the two—Charles and Camilla—were soulmates, resonating with and sharing their love of riding and other activities. The result was an upheaval in the kingdom and the prince's crown was in question.

Had this trio been together before? Were roles the same or reversed?

Perhaps Diana was so desperate to keep the marriage together because she had experienced another royal relationship which had gone awry—one in which she also had been shut out emotionally. Was it past-life pain that added to her desperation? Was this why Charles' friends labeled her mentally unbalanced? Had they tried to remove her before? Was this one more reason why she snuck into the kitchen to eat sweets? Had she been denied food in another castle incarnation because she refused to comply with the program? Had the then-imperials threatened her into submission and silence? Was she held prisoner in her own castle? This time the formerly timid princess fought back—boldly spilling the details out to the media. This time, the princess did not conform to the establishment's expectations.

When Princess Di was killed in a Paris car wreck, the royal family were amazed at the extent to which the princess had won the peoples' hearts. Now it was the family's turn to make concessions. The princess, by example, had shown royalty what true ambassadorialship is all about, how to raise princes who could really help mankind, and how the royal family could become more compassionate while performing their duties. Prince Charles also began to understand the meaning of love and allowed himself to openly love his soul mate, though it was politically unpopular.

The sixteen years from Princess Diana's marriage to her death made a monumental impact at many levels. Had she contracted to be an ambassador of love to her children, her subjects, and the world at large? Had she done this before?

Looking at Princess Diana and Prince Charles' lives

within the framework of reincarnation, we clearly see that the phrase "history repeats itself" takes on new meaning. We can interpret this phrase to mean that some of the historical events may have been repeated. But what's equally significant are the various relationships, issues, emotions, and patterns that may have been replayed.

Although the comparison is speculative, I don't believe lives are haphazard, particularly lives that have influenced the masses. In working with hundreds of clients, I can honestly say that the majority of patterns that emerge in past-life regressions are being repeated again in the present. The value of knowing our past lives usually lies in our ability to get a fresh perspective on our current situation. Against the backdrop of reincarnation, we can have a new understanding of our current reality as one lifetime in a series of lifetimes of repeated patterns and lessons.

Such a viewpoint helps us to grow, expand, and rewrite the past: It's never too late to have a happy past life. By this I mean that we can go back in our mind and reframe our past. We can forgive ourselves and others as we assume that we all did the best we knew how. This attitude is empowering.

After becoming aware of past-life patterns, we often resolve and release the painful memories. This can result in the healing of similar unhealthy, counterproductive patterns in our current life.

In addition, knowing a past life can help us make new healthy choices. Now, we can release our dependence on our old programming and consciously choose life-enhancing patterns. Instead of being like past-life Pavlov's dogs, repeating our outworn habits, we can take more control of our present moments, and, ultimately our futures. This will give us a life filled with more quality.

Finally, having the sense of a direct experience with another time as well as another identity reminds us that we have immortal souls. This, then, is a philosophy of hope.

So, just for fun, look at one possible viewpoint in the past-life scenario I painted about the prince and princess. Could Princess Di have broken old patterns? Yes. In this life she was able to leave a loveless royal marriage, share her vulnerabilities, break out of conformity, speak out, empower herself, get a fair settlement for herself, and still be acknowledged as the people's princess. She was able to raise her beloved sons, find romantic love, feel valued, and become an empathetic ambassador. In life and in death, she became greater than the sum of her lessons because she knew and shared the reason we are embodied: to love.

Could Prince Charles have learned his past-life lessons? Yes. He is learning to share his feelings, love his sons, and love the woman of his heart.

Take another sensational case, that of O.J. Simpson. On June 17, 1994, millions of Americans were glued to their television sets as the football hero and actor, charged with the brutal murders of his ex-wife Nicole and her friend Ron Goldman, led police on a 60-mile chase through Los Angeles before surrendering.

For the next year Americans followed Simpson's televised jury trial as attorneys turned into soap stars.

On October 3, 1995, the jury rendered its verdict: not guilty. On December 20, 1996, Simpson was awarded custody of his two children. February 4, 1997, a civil jury in Santa Monica found him liable in the two deaths.

Two trials, two sets of jurors, two different verdicts. How could we view this national spectacle from a past-life perspective? There are a number of possible scenarios. Let's look at a few.

Scenario number one: The devastated superhero is falsely accused of murdering his wife. Had O.J. been falsely accused of a heinous crime in a past life? Had he paid for a crime he had not committed in the past and this time around he was freed? Had he been rich and famous in the past, able to transcend the law? Had he been saved before from a verdict or situation because of race? Was he murdered by Nicole or Ron Goldman in another lifetime? Had this been a love triangle before?

Scenario number two: The superhero had beaten and threatened his ex-wife on numerous occasions and had been found guilty of murdering her and her friend. Had O.J. murdered Nicole and Ron before? More than once? Had he abused his wife in other lifetimes? How many? Had he murdered Nicole and Ron before, but only after they had murdered him in prior lives? Had he been an abused wife in one or more lifetimes? Was (s)he murdered? Was O.J. falsely accused of murder in another lifetime? Was he falsely accused because of race or poverty, or because he was a commoner?

It is obvious that we could speculate about O. J.'s and Nicole Simpson's possible past lives and never know for sure why their karma played out as it did. But that doesn't make this exercise futile. It serves several functions. The first is to show a number of the past-life options in this case. Some may have more of a ring of truth than others. The important thing is what resonates most to O.J., the Browns, and the Goldmans.

The second function is to bring home to us the fact that, even in such tragic situations, we choose our lessons. Cruel as it may seem, the trio contracted to play these roles in this lifetime, each to learn his or her own lesson. Perhaps they all agreed, before the beginning of their lives, to this catastrophic end so that the world would focus on certain issues, such as domestic violence.

The third function is to understand and apply to this case a very difficult concept: that in the scheme of our many lives, there are no victims and there is no blame. If O.J. had abused and murdered Nicole, had she once, in the distant past, abused and murdered him? Did O.J. get his karmic justice? Apparently he did. Or he will. We cannot judge because none of us can see the larger picture and the trio's set of lifetimes together.

The fourth function is to teach us to forgive and to have compassion. We as a collective—involved because this case invaded our living rooms and our dinner tables—can forgive. We women can forgive the wife abuse. Those who thought the initial verdict unfair can forgive, realizing that the karma was designed that way for a reason. The families of the victims have an incredibly difficult job in forgiving. Addressing this, my only consoling message is that forgiveness is a selfish act that empowers us and frees us from remaining tied to the one we hold a grudge against. Perhaps the most difficult task is for O.J. to forgive himself—for whatever he needs to forgive himself for.

Realizing that we have contracted for or chosen these lessons, that we are making amends or have chosen a part—even if we have taken on the role of bad guy or victim—is empowering. In the universal scheme of soul growth, there is no longer any blame—only lessons it is hoped we have learned.

Both the Princess Di and O.J. stories made impressions on what Carl Jung called the collective unconscious, perhaps bringing awareness about a particular issue to the fore. I also believe that the collective unconscious can be scarred by tragic emotional events of enormous proportions. For example, the American Civil War, the Holocaust, and the Crusades left scars on our composite psyche. As groups and individuals, through a shift in awareness and forgiveness, we can help to heal these collective soul bruises and trauma.

I suspect that reenactors who are recreating the Civil War, World War II, or the Middle Ages are providing themselves with a safe context for healing ancient soul memories. Group reenactments, then, could be one way of healing these group remembrances. Group and individual regressions are another method of melting the frozen blockages of both planetary and individual pain.

By going back to the root cause of the issue that is now manifesting emotionally, mentally, or physically, we are able to free the blocked energy for more joyous living. As it says in the biblical book of Acts, the healing principle is to know the truth and "the truth shall make you free." Often the energy is blocked during a traumatic death.

Even patterns of money problems can be addressed and changed after returning to the root cause. Past-life therapist Joseph Costa, Ph.D. has seen clients with money issues regress to austere lives as monks and nuns. In these situations, past-life patterns need to be altered and current belief systems need to be expanded for the individuals to become successful at changing their lives. Nuns and priests took vows of poverty, chastity, and obedience. Some souls may be clinging to these past-life vows, supposedly made for eternity. Such souls who are not nuns or priests this time around need to rescind these vows, breaking them so that the person can feel deserving of prosperity, healthy relationships, and thinking for themselves. Simply say, "I rescind these vows of poverty, chastity, and obedience once and for all time."

Past lives can also focus on an individual's specific issues and patterns. Dan, a healer-teacher from North Carolina, had bouts of writer's block, feeling overwhelmed by his master's degree thesis. He described writing as "torture." Under hypnosis, he found himself as a ragged monk who felt trapped in a dark, damp cell in a catacomb. Working by candlelight, he had to tediously copy pages of biblical works. Fortunately, his diligence was rewarded by becoming the scribe and trusted employee of a wealthy, powerful official. After his regression, Dan's writing began to flow easier.

Dan's wife, Rio, hates housework. She prefers to travel and teach healing. In a past life, she recalled having been sold as a servant as punishment for speaking the truth. The young woman's spirit was crushed as the rest of her days were filled with boredom and drudgery.

Self-esteem and spiritual issues are also enhanced when dealt with from a multilife outlook. At the end of her medieval regression to France, Karen visited the afterlife. This experience redirected her onto her spiritual path. Several weeks after the regression, Karen claimed to have found a new sense of confidence and support. She felt as if her capabilities and self-esteem had been boosted to a new level.

The primary reason to discover our past lives is not for curiosity's sake but for improving ourselves. Edgar Cayce reminded us of that: "But to know that ye spoke unkindly and suffered for it, and in the present may correct it by being righteous—*that* is worth while!"[2]

Remembering past lives seems to go hand-in-hand with soul growth. Our souls, after all, contain the record of our experiences in the earth. What joy and relief it is to find that there is no irreparable damage from our past lives.

Now is the time to look at the unexplainable patterns and unresolved issues in our lives. Do we ever ask ourselves why, if we had a good upbringing and happy family, do we have relationship problems? Why do we take jobs that undervalue us? Why is life a struggle?

If you can't understand why you are having relationship problems or money issues, or you feel like you are sleepwalking through life, don't despair. If you see toxic patterns that repeat themselves, these may be clues to your past lives. Rejoice! Becoming aware of your clues and your possible past lives begins the process of change. Through your *intent* to heal and through *forgiveness*, you can become a co-creator of your new and improved self!

YOUR PERSONAL BENCHMARK

On a scale of 1 to 10—with 10 being highest—how would you rate your contentment with the following:

1. Relationships, in general   _____

2. Relationship, significant   _____

3. Career   _____

4. Health   _____

5. Finances   _____

6. Home and work environment   _____

7. Emotional outlook   _____

8. Quality of life   _____

9. Self-esteem   _____

10. Current challenge   _____

11. Ongoing challenge   _____

12. Faith in your ability to create your life the way you want it   _____

What issues stand out? Jot down a few key words that highlight these fundamental matters.

A range of 7-10 shows a high level of contentment in that area. A range of 4-6 indicates that you would like to feel more peaceful about a particular area. With a range of 1-4, you may need to give priority to correcting imbalances through gathering past-life insights.

SOUL HISTORY ASSESSMENT

This exercise may give you additional details, insight, and understanding into painful patterns, and soul bruises. Reevaluate your life in terms of:

1. Relationships that were hurtful or dysfunctional

2. Actions, criticisms, attitudes that undermined your self-esteem

3. Events you perceived as failures or disappointments

4. Negative emotions such as feelings of inferiority, resentment, grief, injustice, anger

5. Counterproductive patterns or behaviors such as control issues, fear of intimacy, failure or success, phobias or addictions

6. Did these patterns recur in different phases or areas of your life? For example, growing up and family interactions, school years, marriage and family, career?

Now that you have completed the assessment, your answers will help you to pay attention to your soul's patterns, especially those that may not have an apparent cause in this lifetime. You may want to explore the issues with the most emotional impact first, to discover if there is a past-life cause. After reviewing both exercises, prioritize your most important issues.

Before drifting off to sleep, ask your subconscious for past-life information about one issue, the cause of the unwanted pattern, and whether it was unresolved at death. As you receive answers, whether the next morning or the next month, review them. Imagine changing the life's ending to a more satisfying one. Forgive yourself and others, and ask that the old patterns now be released.

THOUGHT STIMULATORS

• Have you had a situation in your life for which you can find no logical cause?

• Do you repeatedly find yourself in relationships where you are the caregiver, the victim, the victor?

• Do you repeatedly attract jobs in which you are undervalued?

• Do you find yourself having constant money problems? Do you feel unworthy to have or enjoy material things?

• Have certain things come easily to you, e.g., have you achieved goals effortlessly?

• Do relationships or career advances come easily to you?

Woody Allen: His dislike of crowds may have stemmed from a more reclusive lifetime

Clue 10

❂

Physical Reactions, Sensations, Emotions

The smell of fresh-cut grass and watermelon may trigger thoughts of summers past, or perhaps of a lazy afternoon drinking lemonade with friends.

The sound of fireworks exploding nearby may cause us to jump, just as it does for those returning from a war zone. Or the sound might remind us of a childhood celebration in a neighborhood bike parade.

Bare feet touching a wet sandy beach can conjure up a time when we ran reckless and free or sat happily building a sand castle.

The sight of the sun setting over the water can remind us of a romantic moment we shared.

An angry voice yelling in the distance may prompt the

memory of an argument with a family member and a tension in our gut.

Standing near the edge of a cliff may bring a sense of anxiety.

Seeing a snake slither by could stir a feeling of repulsion. Just as sensations, emotions, and physicality can jog our earlier memories, so, too, can they help us recall our past lives.

From the time he was only two Larry repeatedly heard what he thought was a train when he'd go to bed. Forty years later, he identified that sound as one he had heard in a past life in 1876. Larry recalled being Edward Reynolds, a British soldier who was involved in the Battle of Rorke's Drift in South Africa. With the main body of the British army wiped out, thousands of Zulus attacked the remaining small detachment. Larry remembered the British soldiers repelling the natives and he remembered being one of about twenty-four soldiers to survive. The Zulus, who had beat on their shields with thrusting spears to terrorize their opponents, now stood on a hill and again struck their shields—this time in tribute to the valiant effort of so few men.

Some of the strongest sensations and physical reactions we can readily identify in daily life are our fears and phobias. Many fears and phobias originate in our past lives, particularly at the time of death. Fear of heights could presuppose a fall or perhaps being sacrificed and thrown from a temple. A death from a snake or scorpion bite could lead to a fear of snakes and insects in this life. Claustrophobia could have originated by being buried alive.

Woody Allen has had phobias that include long tunnels. Even as a shy five-year-old, he had a fear of being around fellow students. Happier alone, he used to walk through the alley to avoid them on his way to school.[1] As an adult, the incomparable filmmaker's fears have been expressed in his works, which are riddled with angst as well as emotional and psychological issues.

Dusty Waterman, who works for the Association for Past-Life Research and Therapies (APRT) in Riverside, California, said that she gets nervous when she drives through the desert or any place that's hot and dusty. She speculates she may have died of thirst in a desert. Interestingly, Dusty is a nickname for Sandy.

I dislike swallowing pills and they stick in my throat. I suspect that I was poisoned in a former life.

Although being near the ocean relaxes me, I have a healthy respect for it. Whether in the ocean or a pool, I always swim without submerging my face in water. I was told that I was once a mariner who drowned.

I have noticed an emerging pattern in some of my clients and their own phobias. They first noticed their phobias or their fears become worse at about the age they recalled dying from that same source in a past life. If, for example, a fear of flying manifested at twenty-two, that was the same age at which the client recalled being killed in a past-life plane crash.

From the time that Christian, an Atlanta attorney, was eighteen months old, he had a horror of airplane engines. His screams were so piercing that his parents turned the radio up when they heard a plane approaching. One day, he was outside riding his tricycle when he heard an airplane. Panic-stricken, he tried to dig through a stone terrace to hide. His little hands were bloodied by his failed attempt. When he was about five, Christian was sitting in the front seat of a car with his grandparents. As they approached the Cleveland airport, he was filled with terror. He crawled up under the dashboard and once again began digging, pulling out the car's wiring.

Christian's parents concluded that he had probably

lived in a European city that had been bombed during World War I or II. Through time, Christian's condition seemed to improve, and it finally disappeared.

Just as Christian's fear faded with age, Leigh's seems to get worse. Drowning is her biggest fear. As a baby, she had an aversion to boats—particularly steamships—and wouldn't go near the ocean. Growing up, she was fascinated by masted ships and pirate ships and collected books on the *Titanic*. Still, she doesn't trust boats, particularly sailboats, and never sits near the side of a boat. This presented a dilemma since her family lived in Florida and the Bahamas.

While still young, she was watching a television interview of the oldest living *Titanic* survivor. Leigh corrected the story and told her mother, "That's not how it happened." In addition, she "gets the creeps" when she sees water crash onto icebergs or rush into sinking ships. When her boyfriend took the thirty-year-old movie artist to see *Titanic,* such scenes made her so queasy that she couldn't watch them.

Leigh has had dreams of drowning. Recently, Leigh "got the shivers" when she visited the *Titanic* exhibit aboard the Queen Mary and saw its propeller enclosed underwater. Was her fear of water a symptom of a past-life drowning? Ironically, doctors had predicted that she wouldn't survive her birth because she'd have "water on the brain." They were wrong.

Many of these recurring fears and issues can be healed by reliving, resolving, and sometimes reframing the past lives in which the issues originated. We can reframe by reviewing our past lives and changing the circumstances, reactions, and outcomes to ones that are more empowering.

Besides fears and phobias being past-life stimuli, identifying our health concerns is also a stimulus. There is a definite correlation between our physical weaknesses and illnesses and our past lives. Sometimes our past wounds even manifest as birthmarks.

Buddy, a Civil War reenactor, has a history of heart problems. When he regressed back to the Battle of Fredericksburg, he recalled dying after being shot in the chest.

In a past-life medieval battle, Alicia remembers getting a bullet wound in the stomach. Today, the thirty-eight-year-old pharmacist has what the Chinese call a wet spleen. Her digestive problems and migraines are associated with the spleen condition.

In her medieval life, Alicia's male personality underwent surgery without anesthetic. No longer able to be an archer, the soldier then was trained to stitch up people, making him proficient at tying knots. The appearance of an injured child who needed stitching fired an overwhelming anger in the former archer at death and sealed the connection in his mind between death and the tying of knots. In this life Alicia hates to tie even shoelaces. She also can't stand the sight of blood. With that in mind, she chose pharmacy for her career.

In another lifetime, Alicia believes that she was hanged. In this life, she can't stand to wear any type of necklace which puts a strain on her neck.

Often, reliving our past-life woundings and deaths creates healing in this life. During his regression to medieval lifetimes, Nick recalled being beheaded. After re-experiencing his death, Nick said that he was released from debilitating migraines and that his stomach problems receded.

Richard Levy, Ph.D., a clinical psychologist, told a similar tale of recovery. Under hypnosis, a female patient recalled a medieval lifetime in the British Isles in which she had been reduced to prostitution and stealing because of an illegitimate pregnancy. Her infant died of exposure, and the woman died of starvation. This sad story, however, has a happy ending. As a result of her regression therapy, Levy said that the woman's high blood pressure normalized, chronic internal bleeding stopped, and she lost forty pounds.

A weight issue could be an indication of a past life. In her past life regression work, psychologist Dr. Edith Fiore has found that almost all her patients with chronic excess weight of ten pounds or more have had a lifetime where they have starved or suffered extended food deprivation.[2]

Besides physical issues, emotional issues and fears are also indicators of our past lives.

Through her regression experience, Paula said she achieved a new sense of peace. Prior to the regressions, she had been plagued with fears of being physically abused or even murdered. After briefly remembering dying at the hands of a vicious man, she no longer feared being victimized. Her terrors receded.

Besides paying attention to the emotions of phobias or issues surrounding physical health, notice the more subtle clues.

Paula had a flash of a past life while washing her hands after working with red leather. When she watched the red dye go down the drain, she saw herself as a nurse trying to get a musket ball out of a Revolutionary War soldier's leg. "My hands were deep in blood and I could smell smoke, hear shouts, and see cannons."

In the course of compiling remembrances of more than one hundred people who confided that they had a past life during the Holocaust, Rabbi Yonassan Gershom was able to identify some of the past-life triggers.

In his book *Beyond the Ashes*, he reports the memories of a teen named Joan who grew up on a farm in the

Midwest. The young woman had an unexplained fear of barbed wire. After Joan dreamed of dying in a concentration camp, the fear lessened.[3]

Gershom said that in some cases, asthma would manifest when past-life memories were triggered by fears of police, uniforms, and sirens. In several cases, observing Jewish rituals caused breathing problems. For one woman, a blanket activated a concentration camp memory. Several others had a deathly fear of black boots.[4]

Physical and emotional sensations during a regression can also be helpful in determining the validity of past lives. When Dave Morse came back to full awareness at the end of the regression in which he was killed in a Civil War battle explosion, he couldn't feel anything from the waist down. He had to literally pick up his legs to get them to move again.

Some past-life researchers have attached importance to emotional and physical sensations expressed in past lives. Dr. Ian Stevenson referred to an incident in which emotional recollections reproduced actual bleeding at the site of the original wound.[5]

Psychologist Helen Wambach considered feelings the most significant aspect of hypnosis, believing the emotions come from even deeper levels than the visual experiences.[6]

Another element that researchers believe is helpful in determining the legitimacy of past lives involves the vividness of descriptions. Each Civil War reenactor I regressed reported vivid descriptions of his or her regression experiences: surroundings, people, and events. Many descriptions included sounds—bugles, music, explosions. Camps, cities, prisons, hospitals, train rides, fighting tactics, uniforms, and homecomings were all described in detail.

Five reenactors gave physical descriptions of their

Civil War appearance, all differing from their current looks. In fact, David is one of two reenactors who resemble generals, and one of several who look as though they just stepped out of a Civil War movie. In David's regression, he was surprised to find his beard gone and his hair considerably lighter. Most of the reenactors also found they were younger in their Civil War experience.

Dr. Raymond Moody, M.D., focused on vivid descriptions. The regression subjects in his book *Coming Back* said their images were more vivid and real than in ordinary dreams.[7] This vividness of detail, coupled with emotional and physical sensations the reenactors experienced in their regressions, help to support the legitimacy of their regression narratives.

Physical reactions, emotions, and sensations can wake up our past-life memories. They can help us explore the healing of the past lives that they trigger and to judge whether our past-life recollections are real.

The first step is awareness. Take a fresh look at the reactions to what you see, hear, taste or feel that may prompt your past-life recall. Keep an open eye and mind.

THOUGHT STIMULATORS

• Does a particular smell, sound, sight, taste, touch, or emotion prompt an emotional reaction or past-life remembrance?

• Do you have a particular speech pattern, body language, or body structure that could nudge old memories?

• Have you had an illness or pain for which you could not find the cause?

• Do you have any birthmarks? Where?

• Do you have a fear or phobia for which there is no apparent cause? A fear of drowning? A fear of flying? Fear of spiders?

• What was the age you first noticed your phobia?

• Do you have a fear of childbirth? Have you ever had trouble getting pregnant?

• Have you ever had a problem losing or gaining weight?

• Do you have strong physical reactions to certain historic places, events, etc.? What are they?

Martin Luther King:
Did he spend lifetimes setting his people free?

Clue 11

❂

Dreams and Visions

Those who attend the Alabama Symphony Orchestra would never imagine that one of the cellists performs with a cello and bow she's owned in past lives. And yet she believes she does.

JoAnn Strickland plays a Viennese cello that is over two hundred years old—one made by Johannes Christophorus, a student of Amati. Her bow was made in 1930 in Paris by Claude Thomassin. She believes that her current cello was hers in a distant lifetime in England. In that British lifetime, her name was Yvonne North; she was born about 1780 and probably married Francis North III.

But she owned her bow in her most recent previous life. When JoAnn saw the bow in Chicago, she knew that it had been hers and was immediately drawn to it.

Her past-life connection with her bow came to her in a dreamlike state. Prior to the occurrence, JoAnn had gone through the anguish of a divorce and the loss of her job when the symphony shut their doors for four years. Desperately searching for the meaning to her life, she challenged God to show her "without a doubt" that reincarnation existed.

One night, within about a month of her conversation with God, she had what she calls a vision. The digital clock flashed 4 a.m. as a wave of high-frequency vibration went through her body. She felt as if every cell would explode. Then, she saw a clear picture in the area of her third eye. Instantly, she saw the face of one of her past-life children. The child's face was perfectly shaped, but JoAnn had the horrible remembrance that this child and her other three then-children died in a concentration camp in Germany.

Another wave of vibration swept through JoAnn's body. Another picture came. This time it was a picture of a grand piano. JoAnn knew it had been hers and that she had been very proud of it.

When the third wave came, JoAnn feared that her children in this lifetime would find her dead in her bed. This time she saw a handsome man whom she identified as her then-husband. In this lifetime, she had dated this man and, although they never married, they did much research together as a team.

She was visibly shaken. She no longer had any doubt about reincarnation. In the vision, she had learned that she had been a Jewish cellist from Prague who, with her husband and children, was rounded up by the Nazis and put in different concentration camps. She also knew that she had played her cello and died in Ravensbrueck, near Berlin.

She had even received her name, Tess Boros. JoAnn made a trip to the Library of Congress to find a copy of *The Melody Maker*, a magazine about professional European musicians in the 1930s. Not finding copies that went back that far, she persevered and wrote to the British Museum Library. After three months, they replied. Most of their 1930s records had been destroyed by the bombing. Amazingly, however they sent her an article from the 1938 edition in which Tess Boros had written about the Czech composers Dvorák and Smitana. At the bottom of the article was a picture of the woman and her cello with the name "Tess Boros" written under the picture.

In a dream, JoAnn saw Tess in her mother's home in Prague. She remembered being hidden in a closet by her mother as the Nazis stormed the house. The mother allowed herself to be taken so that Tess could be spared. It was JoAnn's current husband who betrayed Tess to the Nazis. JoAnn recognized Tess' mother as JoAnn's current-day daughter. To this day, she says her daughter is motherly and very protective towards her.

The information in JoAnn's initial visions concurred with what several psychics had previously told her—that she was a woman in Europe who had died in the war. It also explained the tone of an article JoAnn had written about Prague composers Dvorák and Smitana before discovering her past life as Tess. It was done in such a familiar style that JoAnn felt as if she were writing about her next-door neighbors.

JoAnn's conviction of her various lifetimes as a musician is evidence of Edgar Cayce's reference to the many lifetimes required to perfect a talent.

Instead of finding her past-life material depressing, JoAnn says that it gave her a measure of hope. She considers the verification of her name and other details as a gift from God. This has given her an inner peace and the belief that all her answers are within. She believes that if she asks, she will receive. "Seek and ye shall find," she quotes the Bible.

JoAnn not only believes in reincarnation, but she now trusts her own truth. This experience has given her strength and helped her to trust and appreciate life. It has affirmed for her that we are not alone, but each is an important part of the Divine Plan in which our lives are closely interwoven.

All her life Carolyn had dreams in which she would create various schemes for killing Hitler. She would inevitably wake up frustrated that she never succeeded. The fifty-year-old pediatric registered nurse from Pennsylvania said that especially after age twelve, she had been spellbound yet repelled by the Holocaust. She read many books on the subject. As an adult, she planned a trip to Germany, then cancelled it because she had such strong feelings against going. At a class on reincarnation, the lecturer suggested that Carolyn may have been a secretary in the Reich who felt it was too dangerous to carry out her plans to kill Hitler.

Carolyn wasn't the only one to find a past life manifesting in her dreams. William, a twenty-six-year-old plant operator from Pennsylvania, saw himself as a nobleman in the British Isles in his dream. Later, a past-life regression gave him more details about "the mystery man." The nobleman was forty-five and dressed in black—from pants and knee-length boots to a black breast plate and cape with fur collar. The noble's lands were prosperous. A foreigner approached about settling his people peacefully on the noble's land. He refused. A battle ensued and although the foreigners were defeated, William's past-life persona regretted his hasty decision.

In this life, William has a history degree, has been fascinated by medieval times, the British Isles, and the movie *Braveheart*. He enjoys talking with a Scottish accent and had used baseball bats for swordplay as a child.

These personal accounts add documentation to the rising number of reported past lives that have been recalled through dreams and visions.

Of more than 120 accounts of spontaneous recall reported by researcher Frederick Lenz, nineteen were the result of dreams. These were different from ordinary dreams, Lenz said, because the dreamers felt sensations, were aware they were seeing a past life, vividly remembered the story when awake, and changed their attitudes about death.

In the book *Lifetimes: True Accounts of Reincarnation*, Lenz tells of an American youngster who was heard speaking French rapidly in her sleep for several nights. The dialogue was taped. A French teacher translated the words which indicated that the little girl was looking for her mother after being separated when her village was attacked by Germans.[1]

Inspired by Lenz, D. Scott Rogo advertised in newspapers for cases of spontaneous recall and got seven which resulted from dreams. Like Lenz, he found them vivid and repetitive and reported that there was a strong feeling these were actual memories.[2]

Parapsychologist Hanz Holzer in *Life Beyond Life: The Evidence For Reincarnation* said that recurrent dreams are inevitably connected with some sort of reincarnation remembrance. In Holzer's opinion, the true test of a past-life memory is that the dreamer sees himself as a participant in the scene.[3]

In *Living Your Past Lives*, Karl Schlotterbeck agreed that dreams can reflect past-life images. He finds that the dreams prior to a regression session are particularly significant and usually relate to a pertinent challenge in the client's life, such as a codependent relationship with a spouse. He frequently uses these dreams as an induction tool for past-life recollections.

If daydreams about past lives are clear, repetitive, and consistent, Schlotterbeck believes they, too, are a good source of past-life remembrances.[4]

In dreams our subconscious minds try to express previous lives to resolve some unfinished business. As long as memories are suppressed, they will not be acknowledged and fully healed. You can begin to pay conscious attention to your past-life memories in dreams. The first step is to be consciously aware that past-life clues are found in dreams.

Secondly, ask—just before going to sleep—to allow past-life information pertinent to your current lives and issues to bubble up to your conscious level.

Third, direct your subconscious mind to remember the images and messages.

Fourth, write down key images, thoughts, or messages upon awakening.

Fifth, ask that the meaning of the messages in your dreams be revealed.

Sixth, ask that past-life healing occur in your dream state and that you will incorporate the wisdom and lessons learned into your current existence.

THOUGHT STIMULATORS

- Have you had recurring dreams or daydreams?

- Are any of the distant past?

- Are any death scenes repeated in a similar way? For example, are you always hanged? Or does your death always occur from trauma to the same part of the body, e.g., a broken neck, shot in the neck, stabbed in the neck?

• Have you or haven't you met the person or persons in these dreams?

• Have any of your dreams seemed to stand out from the others?

• Do you recall any dreams where you felt sensations?

• Do you remember dreams in which you knew you were seeing a past life?

• Do you recognize any dreams in which you were involved in the scene, not just observing it?

• Are there dreams in which you vividly remember the details when you awake?

• Have any of your dreams been instrumental in changing your attitudes about death?

• Have you taken on a different role or identity in your dreams than you normally do?

• Are there any cultural or historic clues in your dreams?

• Have you known details in your dreams that you would have had no way of knowing?

• Do you find the information in the daydreams consistent?

• Do you have any daydreams where the images are clear?

General George Patton:
Was World War II just another toga party?

Clue 12

Déja Vu

The strangest thing happened . . .
. . . on way to the bank.
. . . while I was heading to the baby sitter's.
. . . while I was drinking coffee.
. . . while I was chatting with a friend.
. . . while I was a tourist on vacation.

Sometimes such moments seem out of context—a fleeting glimpse or glimmer of another place or time or person or feeling.

Often, it's so subtle and the events or locations surrounding it are so normal and mundane that we shrug our shoulders and go on without missing a beat. If we don't think further about the occurrence or share it with someone, we might wonder if it really happened. At other times, it can shake us to our core. It's as if a portal opens for a moment, we get a look at another time, the portal closes as quickly as it opened, and we are left mystified. Did the hair stand up on the back of our neck or arms? Did the situation seem familiar? Did we "know" something was about to happen or "know" something we shouldn't have known? If we start to pay attention, we may realize we've had one or more such experience.

In Nancy's case, it was obvious. Nancy, a teacher in western New York, was profoundly affected when she visited Krakow, Poland, particularly the Old Jewish section and the remains of the concentration camp at Auschwitz. As she looked back, she had been preparing for this past-life pilgrimage for thirty years.

As a youngster, any story about the Holocaust engaged her, and she wanted to know more. As a teen, she had read John Hersey's *The Wall* and Leon Uris' *Mila 18*. Although she was raised Catholic, she sought out a synagogue where she felt strangely comfortable.

Her long-awaited trip to Poland was synchronistically made easy, with all the components coming together. Three times her tour book fell open to the Old Jewish section in Krakow. Nancy walked through the old cemetery behind the synagogue. As she wandered among the tombstones, she felt a connection at the deepest level, as if she were revisiting the graveyard.

She also had a sensation of prior knowledge when she visited Auschwitz I. It was the first Nazi concentration camp in Poland, and it was notorious as an extermination center. When Nancy got to "the wall," she knew that people had been shot or hung there. Once she entered the camp, Jewish children were singing holy prayers and

Polish Catholics followed behind her, carrying crucifixes and rosaries. Nancy was intensely moved, more so than her two Polish cousins who accompanied her. She "knew" where Fr. Maximilian Kolbe, a Catholic priest who had exchanged his life for a prisoner's, had been housed.

Down the road was Birkenau, the second phase of the Auschwitz camp. When Nancy went into the tower, she could "see" trains which brought prisoners. Although few barracks remained, she envisioned barracks as far as her eye could see.

When she went into a barrack and ran her hand over a bunk, she was swept with a wave of emotion and intuitively knew that she had slept in that very bunk. Behind the barracks she recognized the remains of a stove, a primitive urinal, and a bathing area. Nancy's visit confirmed her soul union with the concentration camp and the experience.

Since her odyssey, she has had several related nightmares. In the first, she observed Jews disembarking a train, being shot, and thrown into a ditch. A past-life dream expert and intuitive counselor confirmed for Nancy that she had witnessed these deaths in her past life. A second dream involved concentration camp scenarios. By facing her memories and her feelings, Nancy believed that she was processing, healing, and gaining closure on what had been a painful lifetime.

In contrast to Nancy's life events and memories that built on a deeply remembered link to Krakow, the following experience was so subtle and fleeting that I nearly missed it:

If I hadn't been aware of déja vu, I might have dismissed this episode without giving it another thought. I was traveling through a town in southern Spain years ago. When I visited the buildings and monuments that had a heavy Moorish influence, I suddenly felt about eight months pregnant. I lumbered—not climbed—a bank of stairs and was out of breath. Each step I took was more laborious than the one before. Since I wasn't overweight, I thought it was a strange sensation, but I tried to dismiss it. After leaving the town, I immediately felt normal again. It was only in retrospect that I realized I might have been pregnant in that town or another setting with Moorish culture.

Before I had ever given much thought to the Civil War, I went to dinner at a Georgetown restaurant with my friend Barry, who I had just met. As we ate, I was flabbergasted when I "saw" him dressed in a Confederate officer's uniform. Since that time, Barry has become a Confederate Civil War reenactor and I have conducted regression sessions, lectures, and book signings at reenactment battles and as a result of my past-life work. Barry's first uniform pieces were authentic reproductions. He was proud of his slouch hat and butternut pants. I, on the other hand, kept thinking, "He's wearing the wrong hat, the wrong color and he should be dressed in a long gray frock coat more befitting an officer." I had not researched this information. Instead, it was more like an irritant to me, as if something was out of sync.

After several years of reenacting, Barry has become an officer, gotten a hat I "like" and is getting a new uniform. Perhaps we should have past-life designer consultants so that we will get it right the first time. (Or maybe we both had it right if he moved up the ranks and I knew him later when he was as an officer.)

Actually, I do have a past-life designer consultant. My friend Beverly is a costume designer, and she is also very psychic. She has not only seen me as a lady in the Civil War, but she drew a picture of me and the outfit I was wearing. She says that it was a brown taffeta day-dress with a high collar. I wore little net mitts on my hands and carried a handkerchief.

Ironically, the first time I wore my first Civil War dress was at Beverly's Civil War-era house in Port Tobacco, Maryland, where I had gone to regress her to her Civil War life for TV's *Sightings*. After the taping, I had to leave for a book-signing, and so I changed out of my twentieth-century suit.

We replayed one déja vu experience while I visited Beverly's house. Beverly was serving me tea. She was preoccupied with the chipped teacup she was serving me and was worried that I would cut myself. She said we were repeating a situation during the Civil War, when I had called on her at the same plantation site. She remembers that I was a well-connected socialite who was trying to pass her intelligence information by using a coded recipe. Since she had hidden all the fine china from the soldiers, she was distracted by the broken cup in which she had served me.

About eighteen months after his Civil War regression, Buddy Bare, with a fellow reenactor, left a Malvern Hill reenactment to be part of a transport team. As the pair neared the outskirts of Richmond, Virginia, near where routes 5 and 60 intersect, Buddy recognized two old brick buildings. As the truck turned into what had been made into a state park, Buddy's hair stood up on the back of his neck. Exhausted from lack of sleep, Buddy suddenly became energized. He "knew" the site had housed a Civil War hospital. A marker indicated that this had been the location of Chimborazo, the largest hospital in the Civil War.

As the men looked down from the bluff on the two old buildings and railroad tracks, Buddy remembered that he and other wounded Confederates had arrived at the station and been transported up the hill. In his regression, Buddy had been wounded in the Battle of First Manassas and had been sent to Richmond to recuperate before returning to active duty.

Steve Klitsch was a novice reenactor who was brave enough to volunteer to be regressed to see if he could recall a Civil War life while a *Washington Post* reporter observed. That June 1996 night, both the reporter and I sat spellbound as Steve told an emotional story. After the regression, the formerly skeptical reporter told Steve that his experience sounded real.

Fifteen months later, Steve had his first sleepover at a reenactment in Leesburg. In the morning, although Steve doesn't drink coffee, he had a cup of the fire-brewed drink with his mates. Rancid as it tasted, Steve began chewing on the coffee grounds. At that moment, he felt a cold chill run down his spine. This was exactly what he had done as a Civil War soldier in his regression.

The following month Steve joined fifteen thousand men to reenact the 135th anniversary of the Battle of Antietam. Saturday afternoon his unit was amongst the entire Federal force preparing to advance. As far as Steve could see, there were regiments in the field and on the hill. He was hit with a wave of emotions and had to step out of line to compose himself.

The troops reformed for another battle. This time, Steve saw a thirty-piece band playing near a grove of trees. As his men waited their turn to take their position on the field, he watched an artillery team positioning their cannon. Using brute force, the men twisted the cannon, rotating it forward. In a flash, Steve had déja vu, recognizing this scene as one he had witnessed earlier in his regression.

At the 4 a.m. Sunday reveille, men lined up to prepare for the dawn battle in the cornfield. As the troops began their march to the field, Steve saw the black outline of the soldiers against the early blue sky. This scene was exactly as it had appeared in his regression, when he recalled having been an Irish Federal soldier from Boston who fought at Antietam. Later, as he lay on his stomach "wounded," he scanned the battlefield, now strewn with many fallen troops. Again, the tears of an emotional and spiritual connection with the past flowed.

It's not just the Civil War that triggers past-life memories. General George Patton believed that he had been a warrior in many lifetimes. When he arrived at Langres, France, to assume his first command, he claimed to have known where Caesar had pitched his tent and where the Roman temples had been. Patton also recalled being a Tunisian who drank urine from his helmet and cursed the Romans. Once, after being kicked off his horse, he had a flashback of a Viking lifetime. The general described the impact of these experiences as "searing to the soul." When Patton was wounded in World War I, he saw a vision of his grandfather and grand-uncle who had both died in the Civil War.

Daniel Strelsky, an intuitive healer, told me that he's had many déjà vu episodes. He often meets his clients only to feel that for him the conversation and the setting are a replay. He often shocks his clients by telling them personal information he learned from his psychic previsit with them. Perhaps he has worked with these clients in other lives.

When Daniel was eight- to twelve-years-old, his family lived in Okinawa, Japan, where his father was stationed. Young Daniel felt an amazing connection with the island and quickly became fluent in Japanese. Every spare moment, Daniel played serenely on his favorite mountain where he felt he had lived before. A past-life regression as an adult revealed to Daniel that he had been a healer on the island when it was part of Lemuria.

My interviews with some of the radio personalities revealed that they recalled déja vu experiences. Are these
clues to their pasts?

Brian Welsch, cohost on Middle Tennessee's WKXD
rock radio station, told me that he had déja vu at the
Hermitage, President Andrew Jackson's Tennessee home.
Had he known or worked for the former President?

Don't think that we have to be in historical surroundings to experience déja vu. Ryan Patrick, producer of
Z100's weekday morning show, said the simplest objects
or events can quicken that feeling for him—a coffee cup,
the placement of articles, or a conversation. That's a
good point to keep in mind since most of life's daily moments are made up of routine activities.

If you want to enhance the possibility of more and
vivid past-life-related happenings, meditation is one
good vehicle. There are many ways to meditate—from
focusing on your breath to focusing on the words "*aum*"
or "*peace*" to simply clearing your mind in order to be
still.

So it's time to bring déja vu experiences out of the
closet and dust them off. Don't ignore them but pay attention instead. They may give you knowledge, messages, and hints to your intriguing past.

THOUGHT STIMULATORS

• Has a certain place or circumstance felt strangely familiar?

• Does it seem that you have done or said the same things with the same people before the actions actually occurred or the words were actually spoken?

• Have you had a déja vu experience?

• Describe it.

• What stimulated the feelings of familiarity?

• Have you experienced déja vu in a particular historical or geographical setting?

• Have you experienced déja vu in a mundane setting?

Clinton and Lewinsky: Did they transfer their palace intrigue to a White House setting?

Clue 13

❁

Strong Feelings About Someone You've Just Met

Suddenly I stopped what I was doing. CNN news was on, and the news anchor had reported that a congressman had just compared President Clinton and Monica Lewinsky to David and Bathsheba.

Actually, it was a comparison I had considered myself. Whether it was one who sunbathed on her roof in view of the king or the other who flashed her underwear in the Oval Office, in each case the woman played the role of temptress to a powerful ruler. But whether we look back eighty years or 3,000 years, one thing I am sure of—Bill and Monica knew each other before. It was not happenstance that a 22-year-old White House intern would unwittingly do serious political damage to the most powerful man in the world.

There is more here than a determined young woman who headed to the White House to arouse the President or simply a casual friendship for Mr. Clinton. This is not a cosmic, karmic accident.

The most obvious place to look for a possible past-life connection is in Clinton's own domain, the White House. An interesting comparison can be made to Warren G. Harding, the 29th president who was elected to office in 1920.

Though his family struggled financially, Warren Harding grew into a strapping, big-boned handsome youth who played the alto horn. He began his career as a school teacher and later tried reading law. Bill Clinton, who came from a similar economic background and fits Harding's physical description, is a saxophone player and was a law professor before running for office.

Harding's entrance into politics came largely because of his speaking ability. His wife Florence's business ability, ambition and keen mind were driving forces behind his success.[1] He had an easygoing nature and enjoyed golf, similar to Clinton. Both presidents were likeable, intelligent men who had strong-willed women propelling their careers.

As a statesman, Harding was known for his speeches extolling social justice, woman's suffrage, civil rights, and public welfare. The Clintons have followed in some of Harding's philosophical footsteps—working toward a positive impact in the social arena.

Harding's sex life was legendary. Reports were leaked on his serial mistresses. Some say that hush money and intimidation helped suppress even more stories about his mistresses.[2] The Republican National Committee offered one mistress, Carrie Phillips, and her husband $20,000 plus $2,000 per month, a trip around the world, and an extended stay in the Orient for the duration of Harding's presidency.[3]

In defense of her marriage, Mrs. Harding was reported to have thrown a feather duster and wastepaper basket at Carrie, as well as brandishing a heavy wooden piano stool at her.[4] Being more subtle, Mrs. Clinton has used her keen mind and legal abilities to defend her marriage.

As with Harding, several alleged Clinton affairs have been made public. The Gennifer Flowers affair received national attention during his first bid for the presidency. Later, his attorney prepared him for possible grand jury questioning about as many as a half dozen alleged paramours. Clinton's attorneys settled with Paula Jones for $850,000 in a sexual harassment case.

Nan Britton, a young Harding campaign volunteer, was described as pouty, with a chubby but womanly figure and a provocative face. After Harding's death, she published a book claiming he fathered her daughter in a White House linen closet. She had pursued him from the time she was twelve.[5] If Britton's claims were true and if the pair reincarnated as Clinton and Lewinsky, then this might explain why Clinton abstained from having intercourse with Lewinsky.

In addition to both men having affairs in the White House, both had friends or political allies who made efforts, financially or otherwise, to remove the woman in question from the president. Before Britton's pregnancy, Harding had offered her a position in New York so that she could be out of the public eye in Washington but still accessible to him.[6] Later a private investigator, hired by Mrs. Harding, found Nan Britton and her daughter living in Chicago. His investigation showed that Britton had continuously received financial support that appeared to have connections to Harding.[7] Washington insider Vernon Jordan secured interviews for Lewinsky in

New York, and Revlon initially offered her a public relations job.

Nan said that President Harding talked about marriage to her and buying a farm if his wife Duchess died and after he closed his political career.[8] Monica made allusions to wedding talk, although friends believed that such talk was wishful thinking.

In addition to personal scandal, Harding was linked to bribery and fraud that included the crooked real estate deal known as Teapot Dome. C. F. Cramer, attorney for the Veteran's Bureau, committed suicide when irregularities within the bureau heaped another scandal on the pile.[9]

Clinton has been plagued with questions about Whitewater—an alleged coverup related to possible fraudulent real estate loans—and by unanswered questions about the suicide of Deputy White House Counsel Vince Foster.

With the storm of a Congressional investigation threatening to break, Harding—worried and weary—began a cross-country tour. When Monicagate hit the news, the Clintons traveled to Russia.

President Harding died mysteriously in early August 1923 while in San Francisco with his wife and entourage. Although official reports stated he suffered a stroke, rumors circulated that he was poisoned, either by himself or his own wife, to avoid his forced resignation or impeachment. Mrs. Harding's private investigator Gaston Means said the president's wife was "fanatical" about saving her husband's reputation. He reported that Florence Harding returned to Washington and destroyed her husband's presidential papers before attending the state funeral.[10]

If rumors were true that Harding's wife poisoned him, Perhaps Mrs. Harding was attempting to save her husband's reputation and avert the possibility of impeachment or resignation. Whether or not Hillary may have felt like murdering Bill, still she has fought valiantly to save him from impeachment or resignation.

Another potential past-life match with Bill and Monica and their twentieth-century cast of characters could be the court of Henry VIII and his fifth wife, Katherine Howard. Born in 1491, Henry was one of England's most remembered but least popular monarchs. Henry was a gifted scholar, composer, and musician. As a youth, he was carefree and handsome, but later became coarse and fat. He delighted in eating and drinking, although at times he did ride and hunt for exercise.

Bill Clinton studied at Oxford University in England. When he became president, the Rhodes scholar and musician jogged to control his weight. Like Henry who indulged in his meaty repasts, Bill favors a hamburger and french fries.

For twenty-four years Henry VIII was married to Catherine of Aragon, who bore him Princess Mary. In spite of his unfaithfulness, she, like Hillary, stood by her man. Both had been married for at least twenty-three years when their husband's affairs seriously impacted their governmental roles and families. Both women bore one daughter. Interestingly, Chelsea was the name of one of the king's real estate properties.

Henry broke away from the pope and started his own church so he could divorce Catherine and marry Ann Boleyn. When Henry tired of Ann, he had her put to death.

Katherine Howard was one of Ann Boleyn's cousins and a lady-in-waiting to Henry's fourth wife, Anne of Cleves. When Katherine came to court, she was between fifteen and eighteen years old. At least one historian believes that Katherine was coached in the arts of attracting the king before she arrived at court. Henry quickly became enamored of her youthful charms. She was pretty, bubbly, petite, and pleasantly plump.[11] She had sensually full lips and a sweet expression, but she was not without ambition.

While still married to Anne of Cleves, Henry courted Katherine, lavishing her with land and gifts, and he made many midnight boat trips across the Thames to visit her. He called her "his rose without a thorn" and said their relationship rejuvenated him. By the time he married her, he was near 50 years old with a 54-inch girth.

Americans are familiar with the late night trips the 22-year-old intern made to the White House and the gifts that were exchanged with the then-50-year-old president. The personal descriptions of Katherine and Monica are similar. Some news sources even reported Monica Lewinsky's ancestors had a royal British background.

A woman named Mary Hall, who lived with Katherine before Katherine went to court, blew the whistle on the new queen—a role similar to Linda Tripp's. Mary and her brother divulged that Katherine had not been a virgin. They said that by the age of thirteen to fifteen, Katherine had participated in "slumber parties" with several men, one of whom was her music teacher, Henry Manox. In college, Monica had conducted an affair with a married teacher. Katherine also may have been engaged to another man, Francis Dereham; they had referred to each other as husband and wife.[12]

While married to the king, Katherine fell in love with Sir Thomas Culpeper, gentleman of the king's bedchamber. This information became known to Archbishop Cranmer, who used it to sacrifice the queen in the cause of reform. The Archbishop informed the king.

Immediately Katherine and her lady-in-waiting, Lady Rochford, were confined to the queen's apartments.

Hoping to wring a confession from her, Cranmer visited Katherine there and found her hysterical. He offered the king's mercy if she would confess. She did confess to a relationship with Dereham, but the next day changed her story. She lied about her premarital affair and her engagement to Dereham, accusing him of raping her, even though, when the two had been a couple, she had given him gifts that included a collar and sleeves for a shirt made by "Clinton's wife of Lambeth."[13]

These events are reminiscent of Lewinsky's change in the testimony she gave in the Paula Jones' sexual harassment case against President Clinton. At the time, she denied a sexual relationship with the President. Later, in grand jury testimony she reversed that statement. It is also ironic that a lover's gift from Katherine to Dereham was made by an English woman named Clinton.

The queen said she was innocent of adultery with Culpeper. Author Antonia Fraser wrote, "Perhaps the Queen had not—technically—committed adultery, stopping short of full sex with Culpeper . . . Queen Katherine can have been innocent only if the narrowest possible interpretation of the word adultery is used."[14]

Imprisoned in the Tower of London, Henry Manox, the musician, "swore on the damnation of his soul that he had never enjoyed full intercourse with her."[15] After being tortured, Dereham told the Privy Council that he had been engaged to Katherine, but that he did not have relations with her when she was queen.

Even under torture, Culpeper denied full carnal knowledge of the queen, although he claimed that she was "languishing and was dying for love of him" and called him "little sweet fool."[16] Gifts and a love letter written in Queen Katherine's own hand became incriminating evidence. He changed his plea to guilty.

Sound familiar? Even modern American school children have begun to split hairs about the meaning of words following Clinton's grand jury testimony. In these statements Clinton quibbled over the nuances of the meaning of words like "sex." Gifts, love letters, and tapes became incriminating evidence in President Clinton's case. In the tapes, Monica referred to the President as the "Big Creep." He called her "Dear." After his initial testimony, Clinton changed his story, bringing up the question of perjury.

During Culpeper's trial, he claimed that Lady Rochford provoked him to love the queen. The lady-in-waiting's evidence became vitally important because she was an eyewitness and participant, since her quarters were used for the treasonous liaison.

The music teacher was released, but Katherine's other two unlucky paramours were executed, and their heads were stuck on pikes near London Bridge. Dereham was hanged, disembowelled, and castrated while still conscious. Culpeper was beheaded.

Queen Katherine was invited to the Parliament chamber to defend herself, but declined. The Lord Chancellor and members of both houses of Parliament visited her to advise her that she should say something to improve her situation. She declined. She was sentenced to death, taken to the Tower of London, and beheaded along with her lady-in-waiting, Lady Rochford.

The naive young teenage queen's name would become a byword for immorality in Europe. History describes the teenager who was Henry's queen for eighteen months as a harlot and adulteress. As for Henry, it is rumored that he died of syphilis. His sixth wife survived him.

Some of the testimony given in 1542 regarding the sexual relationships of Manox and Culpeper with Queen Katherine are similar to Clinton's 1998 testimony. It's as if he had heard the script before. Could Clinton have been Henry, who had the queen and her lovers judged and murdered? They both had an appetite for women that turned their political "kingdoms" upside down. They were both the most powerful people of their day.

Could Hillary have been Henry's first wife, Catherine of Aragon, who fought against the disruption of their royal marriage? Could Linda Tripp have been Mary Hall who came forward with Katherine's past?

Could Monica's mother, Marcia Lewis, have been her lady-in waiting, Lady Rochford? Monica's relationship with her mother appears to be that of confidante and friend. Lewis shared her Watergate apartment with her daughter. In 1542, Lady Rochford was found guilty of being an accessory to Katherine's crime. Monica's mother kept the dress that became famous, to protect her daughter. Although she had to undergo days of questions by the grand jury, she, like her daughter received immunity. Both were spared prison.

Ken Starr, the prosecutor in Clinton's case, could have been Archbishop Cranmer, who promised the young girl the king's mercy and yet conspired for her downfall. Today, instead of meeting her in royal apartments where she was sequestered, Starr's team met Monica in his mother-in-law's New York apartment.

Was this another case of history repeating itself? Sex . . . scandal . . . lies . . . letters . . . gifts . . . testimony . . . politics. Did the same participants reappear to replay a similar scenario while the whole world held its breath and watched once again?

Ironically, while Clinton impeachment hearings were the subject of newspaper headlines, the same papers advertised a television movie about Queen Katherine who had two-timed King Henry. Coincidence?

Although our relationships aren't followed by the public, many of us have experienced a feeling of "love at first sight." The experience is similar to what's expressed in the song "Some Enchanted Evening" from *South Pacific,* where strangers recognize each other at first meeting. Love at first sight is one kind of instant recognition that we've known each other before. It is usually accompanied by a feeling of comfort and a deeper-than-usual bond. It's as if we haven't seen a friend in several years and then pick up where we left off. Many romances and deep friendships begin this way.

In the case of Dan, he experienced love at first sight in college when he fell in love with Sandy and made plans to marry her. In addition to going to school, Dan also worked for a U.S. senator. When he took the woman he planned to marry to a party on Capitol Hill, Dan introduced her to an ambassador's son. To Dan's dismay, she began dating the son and married him instead. Dan was so devastated that he dropped out of school for a semester.

Ten years later, Dan got the urge to call her. By now she had two children and was in the process of a divorce. They got back together, but her life was still complicated. At a party together, Dan realized that he no longer needed her problems. He handed her a glass of champagne and walked away from the relationship, feeling a sense of closure.

In a past-life regression, Dan found himself a general in the Turkish army. He identified Sandy as his wife. In an underhanded political move, Dan was set up for a fall and was court marshalled. His wife left Dan and married the man who replaced him. In that life, Dan learned humility. In this life, a high point was walking away from Sandy and getting closure.

As in Dan's case, as well as the case of the Clintons and Lewinsky, coming back again with people we have known before can be a painful experience. Sometimes being in love is the hook that involves us in a relationship that will allow us to work through certain lessons.

In some cases, our lovers and friends are there to support and nurture us in our growth and development. In other cases, it's as if some potential lovers and friends are wolves in sheep's clothing. Only after we become attracted to them are the issues and lessons that both parties need to address and resolve slowly revealed.

There are also people we meet and, for no apparent reason, instantly dislike. In the movie *Private Parts*, radio personality Howard Stern claimed he detested one of his producers. Stern's feelings are a strong indication the he knew the producer in a former life or lives.

Linda, a former insurance claims manager in Mobile, Alabama, recalls a time she went into a department store. "The moment I laid eyes on the clerk, she brought up such hostility that I felt like strangling her," she told me. Apparently, the saleswoman also reacted hostilely. Linda's husband, who had accompanied her to the store, was shocked at Linda's abnormal reaction to a stranger.

Have you ever wondered why we are born in a certain place and, as a result, we meet a limited number of people, either where we are or in our travels? Even within our own environments, we gravitate to and interact with a relatively small number of people. Most of those people who make a significant impact on our lives, for better or worse, have been with us before: our families, friends, co-workers.

I pondered our limited interactions when I attended the 135th anniversary of the Battle of Gettysburg. Of the more than 16,000 reenactors, 35,000 spectators, and thousands of civilian reenactors, I bonded with just a few.

One of those was Mac Butler. I had been invited to use

Mac's tent to conduct individual past-life regression sessions. Although I had never met Mac, who portrays Confederate General Heth, he extended a gracious offer. The minute I met him, it felt somehow strangely familiar. In spite of my knowing that he portrayed a general, I would lapse into calling him "colonel." Mac said others did that too. Perhaps, I kidded, we had known him when he had been a colonel.

I also felt very comfortable being in an officer's tent. I knew that I would not be content as an enlisted man's wife. I enjoyed making the acquaintance of all the Confederate officers who came by, as well as those who visited my friend, Union General Mead, who was camped next door.

As I relaxed between battles and regressions, I also began to feel strangely at home with Mac's wife Lisa. Although I was more than half a foot taller than Lisa, several of her long-time friends thought that I was her sister.

While the three of us were still becoming acquainted, I hypnotically regressed Mac. Lisa and I sat in stunned silence as Mac alternately belly-laughed and writhed with pain on his cot. He gestured salutes with his hands, bounced up and down while "riding" his horse, and grabbed his head when he was "wounded."

Slowly, we became aware that he was reliving the life of the real Harry Heth. At times, he almost cried for his men. He also expressed concern for his wife's safety when she visited him on the front. Under hypnosis, he recognized Mrs. Heth as his wife today.

We roused him in time for him to make final preparations to command Heth's Battle, the first of three days of battle at Gettysburg. One hour later, Mac was experiencing the reenactment battle. It should have been thrilling to command thousands of troops on a site near the original battleground. But Mac said it seemed hollow when compared to the carnage he had just seen and smelled and the fear, sadness, and pain he had felt while regressed. Although he doesn't claim to be Heth reincarnated, he admits to having experienced the battle from Heth's perspective.

Lisa and I watched the battle together as we did for Pickett's charge two days later. Although the battles were very authentic and stirring, we also felt that the reenactments were a mere shadow of the horror we had experienced vicariously through Mac's regression.

Lisa and I now occasionally correspond on e-mail, referring to each other as "Sis" or "Cuz" for "cousin," which seems more comfortable. Sometimes she tells me of the new information Mac has "discovered" intuitively about Heth or how he has verified a detail from the regression.

If Lisa had been General Heth's wife, she would have been a belle in Richmond, related to many of the Confederate officers from throughout Virginia. If I had been her cousin, I could have lived in Alexandria, Virginia, and attended social functions with some of the same officers.

My connection with Mac and Lisa at Gettysburg gave me another clue to add to my growing information about my Civil War past life. Our meeting was one more piece of the puzzle I was slowly accumulating, one that, I assumed, happened on cue. Perhaps there was a reason we met at Gettysburg. Regardless, it gave me a lot more to ponder.

Whether or not you can recall any "fireworks" while meeting significant people in your lives, look around. Your meaningful relationships can give you a multitude of clues about a multitude of lifetimes. A word of caution: You may never look at your boss, your children, your spouse, or yourself quite the same way again!

THOUGHT STIMULATORS

• Have you ever experienced "love at first sight"? With whom?

• In what setting did you meet each other? Where and how could you imagine you may have known that person?

• Have you felt a strong and innate dislike for someone, although there is no conscious reason to feel this way?

• How do you get along with them now?

• Do you feel like mothering one romantic partner while another partner may seem like a father to you?

• What significant relationships stand out?

• How would you describe your relationship with each person?

• How are you helping each other?

• What issues do you need to work out together?

• Reflecting on past relationships, what was the importance of your time spent with these individuals?

• Look at your affiliations with groups, such as companies, teams, schools. What affinities, similar beliefs, or goals do you have in common with others in the group(s)?

• What beliefs do you share with these others? Examine your religions, cultures, and countries.

**Oprah Winfrey: She may have known
slavery's history up close and personal**

Clue 14

❂

Preferences and Personalities

S he was blindfolded and dropped off in the Maryland
woods along the underground railroad. For twenty-
four hours, she sat alone, the eerie silence interrupted
occasionally by the clatter of horses' hooves. She would
learn to fear that sound as it meant the arrival of a slave
master who tormented and sexually menaced the slave
woman named Rebecca. Slavery was still a fresh, raw
painful memory. The forty-four-year-old woman, who
was an actor in reality, became hysterical. "So this is
where I come from," she said.

Oprah Winfrey, identified by many as America's most
powerful woman, had enlisted Tony Cohen, the orga-
nizer of Underground Railroad Tours, to create this re-

enactment to help her understand a slave's experience. The scenario triggered memories—not just of Oprah's heritage, but probably of her own past life as well.

Oprah may have thought she was reliving the slavery era so that she could be believable as Sethe, the runaway slave in *Beloved*, the movie that Oprah produced. Recreating a slave's experience paid dividends for Oprah— movie critics described the talk show host as "living and hiding inside Sethe's character."

What might be even more accurate is that, in Oprah's twentieth-century life, Sethe (or another equally feisty African-American, female ex-slave) is living and hiding inside Oprah.

How would we know? Past-life clues Oprah has displayed, even as a youngster, offer the answer.

Oprah, a poor, illegitimate African-American girl, was enthralled with slavery as a child. A descendant of slaves, she garnered courage from slaves' stories of their struggle for survival. While staying on her grandmother's rural Mississippi farm, Oprah read *Jubilee* and other slave books.

As a teen, she often narrated heart-rending characterizations of slave life. The strength she found there motivated her beyond the destiny of many of her race. *Time* magazine reported that Oprah said she had no intention of killing hogs and wringing chickens' necks like her grandmother. She identified instead with the glamorous lifestyle of entertainers such as Diana Ross and the Supremes.[1] Although her father discouraged her, telling her that she wouldn't be able to support herself, Oprah held on to her dreams of being an actress.

In spite of all the naysaying, Oprah became a television news anchor in Baltimore. While there, she read and became obsessed with *The Color Purple*. She bought copies of the book for friends and was consumed with the idea of being in the movie, although she had never acted. Synchronistically, two years later Oprah was working in Chicago when Quincy Jones saw her on television and cast her in the movie's supporting role of Sofia. For her innate acting abilities, Oprah was nominated for an Oscar.[2]

The following year Oprah was overcome when she read Toni Morrison's Beloved and committed herself to a ten-year crusade to bring the story to the movie screen. She was dedicated to exposing and beginning to heal America's race problem by identifying wounds that date back to slavery. She wanted viewers to feel—with their hearts—what slavery was like and then to drop racial barriers.

For Oprah, one vehicle of connecting to her own deepening feelings was her accumulation of slave memorabilia, particularly the property records of various plantations cataloguing slaves by name, age, and price. Throughout the filming of Beloved, Oprah would consult the names of those dead slaves, dedicating scenes to them. But Oprah may discover that the link to her past is even closer than her ancestors; it is her own past life.

For Oprah, who is committed to "becoming more of herself," it makes sense that filming Beloved has been thus far the best time in her life. First, she achieved her dream of filming the book. Second, she was reclaiming and healing her own past life as a slave.

During the filming, she wept when the scars were laid on her back. The corset and bloomers transformed her. Although Oprah admits that in such moments she can get lost in the past, and although she feels the pain, she knows how to acknowledge it, forgive it, and transcend it.[3] In her position as a role model, she is a living example for the healing of the American collective consciousness. Her movie, having reached the masses, is a bright light to assist in heightening awareness.

With awareness comes empowerment. The heavy African-American girl, who was raped at nine, faced her demons both in this life and in her painful past life through acting in *Beloved*.

After she completed one major portion of her soul's mission—the movie and its repercussions—Oprah and her *Beloved* female cast found themselves on the pages of *Vogue*. She said that "as a young, fat girl, she never thought she'd be sitting at the (*Vogue*) table."[4] (Oprah lost weight for the movie. Had she, in her past, nearly starved as a slave, creating her need to eat in this life and constantly struggle with excess weight?)

But *Vogue* was a part of the Big Plan. The now-trim Oprah shed physical and emotional baggage, transcended the pain, and showed all oppressed people that they can be lifted to new, never-dreamed-of heights. This is another manifestation of her personal evolvement and her example to the rest of us. Oprah's search to unravel her past has earned her a "You (and the many you've positively influenced) have come a long way, baby" in the annals of the akashic records.

Just as Oprah relived and helped heal her own and the country's slavery issues through *Beloved*, she could have one final trip back—to her own past life in the slave era. Not only could she relive her own soul's personal experience, but she could have the opportunity, if she chooses, to finally put to rest the ghosts she has discovered. She could also take the leap that would be a role model for all Americans to relive their individual pasts and help to heal race relations.

Oprah's preferences—of seeing the humanity of those born into slavery and searching for self-empowerment for herself and others—are issues that most probably originated in her slave-era past life. Her portrayal of

Sethe, a strong, stubborn personality with grit and tenacity, is similar to the young Oprah, born to unwed teenage parents, who made up her mind she was not going to spend her life on the farm but would make it as an actress. It would not be surprising to find that Oprah's past-life personality is similar to the one she portrayed in *Beloved.*

Author Gina Cerminara tells us that, in trance, Edgar Cayce said we are the sum total of all our past-life memories, manifesting them in habits, idiosyncrasies, likes and dislikes, talents, blind spots, physical and emotional strengths, and vulnerabilities."[5] Because of Oprah's willingness to publicly share so much of herself with us, she has given us a personal illustration of how her very possible slave-era past life has manifested in her current life as a megastar.

As appears to be the case with Oprah's past-life possibilities, many of us "continue where we left off" philosophically and sometimes geographically.

With my interest in metaphysics and the law of karma, I had often wondered whether a Yankee in a past life would reenact as a Confederate, while a past-life Rebel would reenact as a Yankee.

I was surprised to find that only two of the twelve individuals I regressed had past-life recall as soldiers on the opposite side, and both of these reenactors had extenuating circumstances.

Of the two, David Morse rated himself as neutral and said he has considered joining a Union troop in the past. In the other case, Dave Purschwitz was 100 percent committed to the Confederate cause, yet found himself in a Union uniform in his past life. His case was unusual, however, because he recalled being his own great-grandfather.

This consistency in loyalty goes along with what many

past-life therapists find—that thought and behavior patterns recur rather than make drastic shifts. In our twentieth-century surroundings, we continue many of the same affinities we had in the past.

This is not always the case, however. In a regression class with Deepak Chopra, Bernita Stewart, an African American woman from Kentucky, recalled being a Confederate soldier who was shot in the stomach. She believes that her soul chose to return as a African-American female to experience the other side of prejudice and to heal this issue through a new understanding.

Another area where past-life tendencies are expressed is our current degree of masculinity or femininity. Often times, proclivities to homosexuality have been found to have their roots in a past life. Usually in a most recent past life, the individual recalls having been of the opposite gender. In those cases, some of the sexual traits and preferences of the other sex come forward into the current life, resulting in confusing desires and impulses.

Some reincarnationists believe that at times we all change gender. The soul includes both male and female characteristics, and we experience lives as male and female to more fully express both qualities.

Reincarnation author Joan Grant said it's important that we don't deny the instincts and intuition that we acquired as the opposite gender. Instead we should bring those strengths forward into our current life.[6]

MaryLynn Bauer, a civilian Civil War reenactor, recalled being a young Civil War soldier in her past life. She says her friends wouldn't be surprised at that fact because she thinks like a man, is good at plumbing, and had wanted to be an Air Force pilot.

A feminine-looking German woman who lives in Texas found herself in three male lifetimes. In the first, Sigrid's past-life persona was leading an army to the Holy

Land during the Middle Ages. During a battle he was slain with a dagger. As he slumped to the ground, Sigrid could feel the warmth of the cobblestones below the body. The leader's son was taken to safety, and his wife wept over the body.

In another life, she recalled being a farmer, clearing land in Pennsylvania and owning a nice horse. The man became involved in George Washington's fight for independence.

In a third life, Sigrid was a gold digger on his way to find his fortune with a donkey and shovel. Without making it to his destination, the man died in the salt flats within view of snowcapped mountains.

Another strong woman, WRKO Boston radio host Leslie Gold claims she doesn't like clingy guys and she's not a clingy woman. Still, she warms up to men rather than befriending women. She dislikes sharing her feelings and talking on the phone and considers women whiny. A male past life? Possibly, although Leslie, like MaryLynn, is secure in her femininity.

Besides sexual preferences, personality traits, talents, and other preferences can continue from past lives.

College student Heather Heath is a natural horsewoman. The Youngstown, Ohio, woman consistently placed in the top ten in her state in Western Horsemanship and Western Pleasure, which rates the horse's performance. While touring Avebury, a Stonehenge-like site of massive standing stones near Glastonbury, England, Heather had a flash of being on a horse that was killed when a sword was thrust into its chest. Heather became nauseated at the sight and sensed that she may also have been killed. She recognized her horse as the one she had competed with in this existence.

Although Craig, a baron in the SCA, reenacts as an Irish-Welsh persona, he also reenacts as a Mongol. He is a member of the Dark Horde Moritu, which portrays thirteenth-century nomads during the reign of Genghis Khan.

While many members of the SCA portray characters who are similar to their cultural heritage, others like Craig delight in portraying characters who are culturally different from their present heritage. Besides his early interest in Arabic cultures, is there a Mongol lifetime lurking in his distant past?

Rookie Civil War reenactor Alan McBride described fixing his focus in reenacting on being a "spit-and-polish" soldier. He is a stickler for grooming and always looks immaculate in his uniform. His presentation and marching are top priorities for him. Ironically, in his past life he remembered being a disheveled prisoner-of-war who admired the orderly, pulled-together uniformed guards.

Even though Alan hadn't previously known much historic detail, I found what could have been the personality he recalled under hypnosis, in the National Archives. A Sergeant Edward White of Company D, 13th Pennsylvania Calvary had, just as Alan had recalled, been released from Salisbury Prison.

We've looked at a range of preferences and personality traits—from Oprah's passionate attention to slavery to a partiality to reenact a particular side in the Civil War and from the carryover of abilities of a prior gender to character strengths, natural capabilities, and predilections.

Now it's your turn to look within and continue your self-discovery process. These new clues to your past lives should uncover and flesh out information that may be revealing and ultimately helpful to you.

THOUGHT STIMULATORS

• Do you feel more empathetic toward one race, group of people, a cause? For example, have you leaned toward supporting the Union cause even though you grew up in the southeastern United States?

• Do you have strong views about an issue and yet don't have any logical reason to substantiate it? For example, do you always fight for the underdog?

• Observe your reactions to what you see, hear, and read.

• Do you have leanings towards a sexual preference that is not the norm? Do you have a rational explanation for it?

• Do you like or dislike a group of people, such as people in leadership roles, for no apparent reason?

• Do you have any peculiar emotional responses to specific circumstances or events?

• Do you have any blind spots or biases?

• Are you particularly vulnerable to something or someone? For example, are you vulnerable to criticism? Criticism by a particular person?

• Are you drawn to a certain deceased relative? Do you exhibit any of the same physical or personality resemblances?

• What personality traits or habits are particular to you

but not evident in the rest of your family?

- Do you have any idiosyncrasies?

- What are your physical strengths? Shortcomings?

- What are your emotional strengths? Shortcomings?

- What are your likes? Dislikes?

The Marx Brothers:
From court jesters to stand-up comics?

Clue 15

❂

Joking About Past Lives

Atlantis. The golden domed-and-columned temple was surrounded by lagoons which spilled into waterfalls. Fish of every species swam lazily in the pools. Tall trees swayed slowly in the soft breeze. Flowers of every color were abundant. Out of nowhere, music wafted along the winding garden paths. A white sand beach rimmed a portion of the garden where the ocean lapped on the shore. In the sunlight, it was beautiful. But in the darkness, it took on an ethereal and mysterious quality. A tropical paradise!

Inside, it was relatively quiet. I sat at a table waiting for a friend who was late. A stranger approached and asked if he could join me. I nodded. I was enjoying an evening at the Atlantis Hotel, Paradise Island in The Bahamas—a resort inspired by the myth of the Lost Continent of Atlantis which vanished, some think, in the ocean beneath the Bahamas. The stranger made me laugh so hard that my sides ached. Mickey Dean, this new companion, was the comedian booked to entertain at the palatial Caribbean resort across the bridge from Nassau.

Mickey, from Birmingham, Alabama, was born to tell jokes. I admired his ability to see the funny side of life and poke fun at the everyday events and circumstances of peoples' lives. But I was equally interested in the philosophy of humor. I had always believed the old adage, "half in jest, half in earnest." In fact, I have observed that there is usually a ring of truth in peoples' humor.

Mickey confirmed my suspicions. He told me that people have to relate to a joke in order for it to be successful. If there isn't a kernel of truth in it, people won't relate to it. In addition, although it didn't apply to him, Mickey told me that some comedians have had unhappy childhoods and that they used humor as a coping mechanism. No doubt it is also an attention-getter.

I had known that some comedians fell synchronistically into their roles. Gracie Allen was an example. As a youngster, she did a vaudeville act with her three sisters at the Hippodrome. While the Four Colleens did their song and dance routine, Gracie accidentally slipped on talcum powder on the stage, pulling her sisters down. The audience roared with laughter. This unplanned mishap was the beginning of her career as a comedienne that spanned more than forty years.[1]

A similar scenario involved the Marx brothers. During one of their early performances, a disturbance took place outside the theater. Rather than lose their audience to the excitement outside, they became quick-witted and caustic, creating a style of humor that followed them throughout their careers.

I told Mickey my belief that there is some truth behind our joking about past lives. When we joke about a past life, the information comes from the subconscious. But since reincarnation has not been part of the norm in Western thinking, we censor these past-life details, filtering them through humor. That way, no one has to believe it, least of all us.

I had seen this concept demonstrated in my own life. For many years, I had kidded my younger sister, telling her that "I must have killed you in a former life." Several years ago, she stayed with me while she attended a conference. I offered to do a regression for her, and she recalled being a Native American child separated from her family after being captured by another tribe. When she was old enough, she set out on a search for her family and found them. Not only was she reassimilated into her original tribe, but the leader's son also fell in love with her. I, her then-older-sister, was jealous of this liaison and conspired to have her killed.

I was shocked. Fortunately, I believe that we should look at our past lives in a nonjudgmental framework—a touchstone from which to learn and grow. I had to admit that my sister's recall was a tough pill for me to swallow, and I have had to make up for it ever since.

On a more uplifting note, ever since I was young—and decades before I had ever heard of reincarnation—I used to think of my dad as a "philosopher-prince." It seemed strange to me and I could never understand why. Looking back, I found it a revealing coincidence that my uncles had also referred to my dad as "the prince." In recent years, it has dawned on me that my dad, whose refined yet humorous personality was respected, may have been a real philosopher-prince in a past life.

Jolen Chang, one of my friends and a metaphysical minister in Virginia, remembers saying, only half in jest, "The stork made a mistake when I was dropped off in China instead of Britain." Jolen never related to her Chinese culture and always gravitated to anything British. She said, "Who else gets excited over the words 'brambles' and 'moors'?"

Through the years Jolen has read everything she can about the British Isles. One of her special interests is the Cornwall area in Southwest England. The isolation and the sea battering against the cliffs remind her of a past life there. In it, her sparsely furnished house was perched on the side of a bluff. She saw herself as a severe-looking woman in a plain dress. She was distressed because she had wanted to write about her feelings and women's issues, but her husband had forbidden it. In a final scene, she witnessed her husband's distress after she jumped to a watery death. In this life, she has been told that she needs to be published.

Another special area of interest is the King Arthur legends. Jolen says, "If there was a King Arthur, I was there." She's read just about everything that's been published on the topic. The written page transports her back to the time where cold castles and rushes—reed-like plants that carpeted the floor—feel strangely familiar. Sometimes, she says, she can even hear the sound of feet against the rushes. Jolen envisions herself as a lady of the court and can even taste the food served from large platters.

Today Jolen loves heavy tapestries, shawls with woven designs, and flowing dresses. One Halloween she appeared as Merlin in a green hooded robe with an owl on her shoulder. She has also named a plant "Merlin," her car "Camelot," and would name a pet "Lady."

One of Jolen's frequent phrases is, "It's a medieval torture." She recently referred to an old can opener that was hard to handle as "a tool of medieval torture." Recognizing that she is simultaneously pulled and repulsed by the medieval times in the British Isles, she is aware that the concept of torture particularly upsets her. She has been told that she was a torturer and a tortured victim in those past dark ages.

Joking that he had been a court jester in a past life, Tee Morris had déja vu at a museum in Washington, D. C., that reinforced his humorous past. The chamber's walls were lined with Mediterranean-style tapestries, and a massive banquet table and old chairs filled the room. Feeling as if he had been there before, Tee flashed back to a scene of a dimly lit great hall with a roaring fire, saw himself making people laugh, and even heard raucous laughter.

Later, in one of his past lives recalled under hypnosis, Tee discovered he had made his living as a court jester, blowing fire and juggling. He was wearing a bright red-and-yellow outfit and had bells on his hat. He died of the plague a year after being married. These days, his persona at the Maryland Renaissance Faire is a humorous one.

Civil War reenactor Dave Morse used to joke to his friends that he must have died early in the war. He felt that he must have died by 1863 because he had no emotional connection with the battles beyond that time. Prior to that, he resonated deeply with the earlier campaigns.

In his first regression session, Dave went right to his death in the Civil War. He had to return for a second session so that we could determine what had happened up to that point. Shortly into his regression, he returned to a dramatic death scene.

At his death, Dave had recalled being George Henderson,

attached to Company K of the 2nd Rhode Island unit. According to historian Brian Pohanka, 2nd Rhode Island was one of the first regiments to leave the state for the war. It was heavily engaged in the Battle of Bull Run in July 1861 and sustained heavy losses. Dave could have been killed in the war's first battle.

Dave's past-life description was also similar to 2nd Rhode Island's march down a road to the Gettysburg battlefield during which thirty men were killed or wounded.

Dave's joke may have been no laughing matter.

Here's another perspective on death and past lives. Carmen's father used to kid her about having been his mother. Carmen was conceived two months after her grandmother died. She is now fifty and a nurse. At least fifty times since her father's death in 1995, his photo has fallen off Carmen's roll-top desk and has been found facing in the direction of her grandmother's picture. Was Carmen's father confirming his jests about her prior life, from the other side?

Alan Alda, the actor, subscribes to this definition of comedy: "Comedy is tragedy and time." This is an interesting definition of humor, particularly when examined from a past-life perspective. Many of the things we joke about now or use repeatedly as familiar sayings were not funny, but tragic, when the events occurred.

Besides information from the subconscious that we "repackage" as humor, there are phrases that we use as if they are "throw away" sayings or expressions of emotion that have little or no meaning.

For example, we may often use these expressions: "This really burns me up." "I am drowning in this." "The boss treats me like a slave." "My husband treats me like a queen." "I can't stand this." "I'm all choked up."

Actually, Morris Netherton found his clients could tap

into past lives through repeating emotionally charged phrases like "I'm seeing red." He is credited with developing a way to elicit past lives without hypnosis. His work has greatly influenced professionals who have incorporated or adapted his methods.[2]

To sum it up, pay attention to stock phrases that you say frequently. Notice humorous references to past lives and repetitive clichés and expressions. They may be truer that you think!

One final word in connecting humor and past lives: We should recall the words of Hester Mundis, who gave us *101 Ways to Avoid Reincarnation:*

> If you knew you were once:
> Hannibal, you'd never make mountains out of molehills.
> Joan of Arc, you'd want nothing more than to stop smoking.
> Ann Boleyn, all you would think of is getting ahead![3]

THOUGHT STIMULATORS

• Have you ever joked about doing something or being someone in another life?

• Have you ever kidded about a relationship with an individual that you may have had in a former life; for example, "You must have been my big brother before"?

• Can you look at your current relationships and imagine that your roles were different in the past? For example, could your boyfriend or husband now have been your son or husband before?

• Do you repeat phrases, such as, "My boss treats me like a slave," or "It really burns me up when . . . "? What are such phrases and when do you use them? Does a particular circumstance cause them? What type of past life could elicit such a comment today?

• Have you given or been given any pet names that seem to have no bearing on the present? What are the names? Where might they have originated?

**Elvis: The King was fascinated with The Sheik;
coincidence or past-life synchronicity?**

Clue 16

✿

Synchronistic Experiences

Imagine stepping out your front door and seeing your favorite movie star. Right outside my Alexandria, Virginia, condo sat Harrison Ford, being made up for a movie scene, in a white limo. Although I had met movie stars and celebrities as an international flight attendant based in Los Angeles and later as a reporter and news anchor, I hadn't seen one recently in my Virginia neighborhood. Besides, I was writing a screenplay, and he *had* to play the male lead. I couldn't have dreamed up a better synchronistic experience in a million years! (Synchronicity is a "meaningful coincidence or simultaneous occurrence," and this was meaningful!)

There was only one hitch. I was on the phone when

he was outside. When I came out minutes later, I was told that I had just missed him! Talk about being in the right place at the wrong time! I guess my stars weren't aligned that day. This *could* have been one of my all-time best synchronistic experiences but, without the universe's help, it missed its mark and was relegated to the category of a regret. Its lack of synchronicity reminded me, however, not to take for granted meaningful synchronistic experiences where everything does come together effortlessly, as if by magic.

A superstar who was aware that "chance" events weren't chance at all was the country boy who got his start in Memphis.

Elvis Presley was the king of synchronicity—a great believer long before the term became popularized. He used to tell his friend Larry Geller, "You know, there are no coincidences. There's more than meets the eye." In response to a reporter's question about the reason for his incredible success, Elvis answered, "because God let me come along at this time."[1]

The grandson of two sharecroppers, Elvis became a legend by age twenty. Because of his poor upbringing and his instant success, he had to ask himself, "Why was I chosen to be Elvis?" He felt as if he had an unseen hand behind him, guiding him. He looked for the true meaning in everything and knew that there was a purpose for his life.

Elvis was mesmerized by the century's first male sex symbol, silent screen star Rudolph Valentino. Could it have been coincidental that Elvis became fascinated by Valentino's legendary power over women and the cult that arose around Valentino after his death? Could Elvis, who was too shy to admit that he was his own generation's sex symbol, have imagined the many fans who would revere him long after he had died? Since Elvis looked for the true meaning in everything and believed in synchronicity, what might he have thought about his similarities with Valentino's most famous character, the Sheik, including a vague physical resemblance? In *Harum Scarum*, Elvis even wore the Sheik's trademark costume.[2]

In 1953, Elvis paid four dollars to record his first record. The studio assistant liked his style and encouraged her boss to call him. Her boss did. One year later, Elvis recorded "That's All Right." It was an overnight smash. A lucky break for a small town kid?

There are other "lucky break" stories among the Super Great. From time to time we hear of a model who was discovered on the street, an actor who played hookey from school and was discovered in a park, or an understudy who got a break when the lead was sick.

Lana Turner's story is the classic case. She wasn't out doing casting calls when she was discovered. Lana was at a soda shop in Hollywood when the right person told her that she ought to be in movies.

Although Elizabeth Taylor's mother Sara had been a Broadway actress and put her daughter in dancing school at an early age, Elizabeth did have a few synchronistic encounters which placed her on the road to stardom. By the time she was seven and the family lived in England, Elizabeth was already showing signs of being a talented ham. A client of Elizabeth's father, an art dealer, even arranged for the young girl to dance before Princess Elizabeth.

Later the family moved to the Beverly Hills area. One day, a prospective client visited the art gallery and was enamored with Elizabeth's beauty, her voice, and the way she walked. The visitor was the wife of the chairman of the board of Universal Studios. Elizabeth's British accent set her apart from the other child actors. In short order, Elizabeth was under contract and was cast in *Lassie*

◆

Come Home. Her riding abilities, developed in England, clinched her role in *National Velvet*. By fifteen, her career was established. Were these contacts, her mother's acting background, the accent, and the abilities Elizabeth had developed just breaks, or was she meant to be a star? [3]

A serendipitous accident or chance event? Many of us would consider Elvis', Lana's, or Elizabeth's stories as lucky breaks. Perhaps their desires were tapping into Jung's collective unconscious. Or maybe they were dipping into a huge pool of universal energy and attracting circumstances and people to which they resonated.

Conceivably their fame and recognition were earned from other lives. Even though celebrity status was their destiny, each star had to consciously choose that path and apply their skills. Perhaps it was no accident that Elvis, Lana, and Elizabeth went on to become stars. Was Lana following her intuition or higher guidance to go to the coffee shop that day? And even though Elizabeth got discovered by the wife of a studio board chairman, she had the talent and determination to follow through. Perhaps it is not an accident that child stars choose to be born to mothers who become their stage mothers.

The message from all these stories is that when we pay attention to them, synchronistic events can help to verify or give us clues to a past life.

One incident that nearly brought tears to my eyes occurred when I was trying to verify the Civil War past-life identities that the reenactors recalled under hypnosis. If any reenactor had been a single number off in remembering his unit, sifting through the National Archives records could be like finding a needle in a haystack. When I approached an archivist for help, he tossed me a book on a Southern prison in an effort to get me quickly out of his office. It fell open and as I looked down, I saw one of the matches I needed.

Since then, I've heard of numerous "coincidences" that help to verify regression information. During his regression, Dave Purschwitz remembered the Civil War through his great-grandfather James McNally's eyes. A year after the regression, he accompanied a *Sightings* television crew to the site of the Battle of Piedmont where he, as his great-grandfather, was wounded and lost his arm. There he unknowingly retraced his past-life steps. Months later, a researcher of the battle's troop movements lectured where Dave worked. The lecturer's new research indicated that McNally probably was shot where Dave had experienced it in his regression; the research showed McNally's troop advance as farther than had previously been thought by historians.

There are more coincidences when Dave's life is compared to that of his great-grandfather. When Dave started his own reenacting unit, he chose Company F, 8th Virginia Infantry. Years later, he discovered that McNally had been with Company F, 8th U.S. Infantry.

Although Dave was a regimental commander for twelve years as well as brigade commander, he prefers being a private. James McNally enlisted as a private and remained a private throughout his military career. James McNally was born in Ireland and moved to New York. He died in Maryland five miles from where Dave was born. Dave was born exactly one hundred years later and was in the Air Force exactly one hundred years after the Civil War.

Ed Embrey, another reenactor in Dave's unit, had a synchronistic occurrence that helped to verify his regression. One thing that had puzzled Ed was a scene in which he was a prisoner at Elmira, New York. He couldn't understand how a little girl who was up above him could have thrown down a carrot to him.

Within weeks of his regression, Ed was in Fredericksburg, Virginia, looking for a book on prisons. Having no luck, he picked up a book entitled *The Photographic History of the Civil War.* The book fell open to a picture of a twelve-foot walkway on the outside of Elmira's prison wall. Soldiers charged civilians ten cents to climb up and see the prisoners.

Wally Holderness, a federal reenactor, consented to be regressed for Fox television in Washington, D. C. Not only was he an excellent subject, but he also recalled under hypnosis being a Confederate deserter. To me, this made a great case for reincarnation because no one would make that story up while a television camera taped it.

Serendipitously, Wally found a book about the 15th Missouri Cavalry regiment he had recalled in his past life. This confirmed his recalled name, Joshua Anderson, his unit, and other details, such as the fact that he was recruited from Jefferson County and sent as a scout to Kentucky. Unknown to him in his current life, the Missouri Independent Scouts were sent east to help defend Columbus, Kentucky. Under hypnosis, Wally also referred to "the bluff." The 15th Missouri, commanded by Colonel Johnson who was mentioned in the regression, was involved in the Battle of Chalk Bluff. When Wally's Civil War personality decided to desert, he said that he'd have to get through Price's army in Arkansas. He confirmed that General Sterling Price was commanding Confederate forces in Arkansas at that time. All of these facts were unfamiliar to Wally prior to his regression.

Sometimes synchronistic happenings help us find our mates. Regression therapist and author of *Journey of Souls: Case Studies of Life between Lives,* Michael Newton, Ph.D., recognized three clues that helped him find his wife. When he was a teen, he was flipping through *Look* magazine and was drawn to an advertisement of a

Hamilton watch modeled by a beautiful dark-haired woman in white. The caption said "To Peggy." Years later, on his twenty-first birthday, Newton's favorite aunt gave him a Hamilton watch. While in graduate school, Newton was washing a load of white laundry when he got the message that it was "time to meet the woman in white." Heeding his intuition, he headed to the largest hospital and asked for a woman who fit the model's description and was named Peggy. He met his future wife, who was just getting off duty and bore a striking resemblance to the *Life* magazine model. During their first meeting, he felt as if they were old (past-life) friends; she knew he was her husband-to-be.[4]

In many cases like Michael Newton's, synchronicity can best be appreciated when we look back and see the impact of the synchronistic event or series of events in retrospect. At this point, several of the puzzle pieces or clues may have come together to give us a larger framework from which to view our lives. External events remind us that we are on course and that our lives seem directed, not purely happenstance. It's as if a veil has lifted. We can then keep on the path we have set for ourselves prior to our arrival in this life—a course partly predetermined by our past lives. At such significant moments, our amnesia is erased and we are given glimpses of our path and guidance from our spiritual helpers and higher self.

Nora's story of relocation is a fascinating succession of such episodes. Her first message came to her via a Ouija board in 1987: "Go Chalotsville." When she asked why, it said, "You were his children." This convinced Nora, who is of Russian Jewish ancestry, that she had been one of seven children of President Thomas Jefferson and Sally Hemings, Jefferson's African-American slave who Nora believed had been with him for thirty-eight years—from shortly after he was widowed until his death.

Compelled to pursue the Ouija board's message, Nora checked out a library book on Sally Hemings. By coincidence, the book had been written by Nora's classmate at Yale Arts School, Barbara Chase-Riboud. Nora's reaction convinced her that she had been Beverly, a son and the fifth child of Jefferson and Hemings. According to Nora's research, Beverly had a private tutor and access to Jefferson's books. The red-haired, blue-eyed Beverly left Monticello at twenty-two, married a white woman, and disappeared from history.

Coincidentally, Nora was raised on stories about Jefferson. Her uncle Fred, a Jefferson scholar, lectured to her about the Founding Fathers until Nora tired of hearing about these men by age ten. Later, Fred, an immigrant from Russia, raised funds from American school children who donated five cents to help buy Monticello from private owners. In her twenties, Nora became a Jefferson fan when she first visited Monticello and saw the President's talents as an architect, designer, and horticulturist.

In 1991 she decided to relocate and found that the Charlottesville area met her requirements. In what appeared to be another destined event, the property she bought was being auctioned for half the original asking price at the moment that Nora was looking to buy. The property was next door to Monticello and had originally been part of it.

Since she has lived in Charlottesville, Nora has met several others who know they once lived at Monticello. The first caretaker of Nora's property may have been another Hemings. Before meeting Nora, he was told by a psychic that he would meet someone named Nora who would change his life. When he first moved onto her property, he said, "I'm home at last."

When I met him, he was not only the caretaker of Nora's property, but also a chef. When I regressed him, he recalled standing over a hot stove and feeling resentful that he had to remain a slave at Monticello. He recalled being Sally Heming's nephew, the chef, Peter. His then girlfriend, now wife, was Sally's sister Critta. Living on the same land with another person who recalled being a Hemings on the Jefferson plantation was a confirmation for Nora that her own memories of a past life as Beverly Hemings may have been correct.

I find it interesting that tourists from around the world wait in line for hours to see Jefferson's home but neither Nora nor her caretaker have stepped one foot inside the neighboring grounds of Monticello. Both have been healing. Both, now white, were still enraged by the slavery issue. But with time, compassion, and understanding, Nora feels she's healed those lifetime memories.

Nora is an astrological researcher. Her teacher, before he died, taught her a secret method for confirming past-life reports. Her chart yields: "Son of a chief," but also "slave." One last synchronistic detail has helped Nora heal her past life as a Hemings. She met a woman she describes as belonging to Virginia gentry. The woman said she had been at Monticello, too. At age five, the woman recalls being in a nightgown and watching a Monticello dinner party from the stairway. She also recalls playing on the lawn at Monticello. Nora believes this woman is Polly, Jefferson's legitimate daughter. She is Nora's best friend in Charlottesville. Nora speculates that "Polly's" husband in this life was once Meriwether Lewis, one of a pair of explorers commissioned by Jefferson.

Nora believes many who were around Monticello at the time of Jefferson are being drawn back to Charlottesville. Synchronistically, during the writing of this chapter, it has come to light that DNA testing of one of the Hemings family descendants shows that it is very likely that the Hemings were Jefferson descendants.

So we can see the saga of synchronistic events that showed Nora she was on the path to rediscovering and healing her past life as the son of a remarkable man. Nora's mindfulness of her synchronistic experiences can inspire us to pay attention to these dramatic glimpses and sometimes fleeting, but meaningful, moments. By acknowledging them when they happen, we can begin to recognize the gift of understanding that is given. When things appear to "click in," this is outside confirmation that we are on track. As we, like Nora, incorporate this wisdom into our lives, we will begin to look for patterns and see the cohesive nature and the clues that such patterns bring concerning our past lives.

THOUGHT STIMULATORS

• Can you identify any synchronistic occurrences?

• Where did they happen and with whom? Did you learn anything from these chance events?

• Can you recall any chance happenings involving relationships, career, or your living situation?

• Can you see a pattern of meaningful experiences?

• Can you see a pattern of seemingly inconsequential events such as messages on license plates, repetitious numbers on clocks, affirmations that come from television or other people?

• Have you had what you might classify as a lucky break? In retrospect, what did you learn from it?

• As you begin to formulate one of your past lives, does something synchronistic (a simultaneous occurrence) happen to verify that possibility?, e.g., If you decide you may have lived in Northern Italy, does a friend invite you to Cafe Milano for a cappucino?

**Elizabeth Taylor: The hair, the jewels,
the *Cleopatra* role—maybe she'd done it all before.**

Summary

❁

How to Interpret Your Clues

Bits of blue sky. And lots of green. That's all it ever looked like to me. My older brother, Jim, amazed me because he patiently took these small puzzle pieces, strewn across a hobby table, and fashioned them into a cohesive landscape.

I had neither the aptitude nor interest for those cardboard puzzles. Even so, I was always intrigued with the most seemingly inconsequential hint that would suggest more insight and understanding into myself, others, and human nature as a whole.

In recent years, my friend Barry has told me that I'm like a Mayan because I read a meaning into everything. I've slowly came to believe that even the simplest thing, like the choice of an outfit or a street name, can be significant. Not to mention the big signs like being zapped with a love-at-first-sight feeling or walloped over the head by a painful pattern.

The dimension of past lives added to my fascination. I had been a history major in college, but I had never seen the concept of history repeating itself with such unmistakable clarity until I became a past-life regression therapist. With each client, I saw history repeating itself—in talents, activities, thoughts, and behaviors. The regressions heightened my awareness that history is about real people. These very real people, individually and collectively, repeat patterns over and over. Understanding this, I could see larger historical patterns that emerged to be repeated again and again.

Gradually, I began to personalize this awareness. No longer do I shift restlessly while a historian talks about people, long gone, who I once thought could never have meaning to me. Now I look at the photographs hanging in historic sites as if I were seeing real people. But it's my own past-life exploration, rather than my history teachers, that moved me toward this understanding.

To help you recognize and piece together clues to your own journey through the past, let's look at the past lives of two people through the clues presented in their current lives. You may begin to see how your past lives have been entwined with the significant people around you this time.

As a young boy, Mike spent the humid summer nights at his grandparents' farm falling in love. The fragrance of the newly-mowed alfalfa hay wafted up to the second floor bedroom where Mike lay in an old oak bed gazing at the watermark-stained ceiling, 1930s floral wallpaper, and two massive portraits of his great-great grandparents staring sternly down at him.

In stark contrast to his austere ancestors imprisoned in their heavy carved oak frames was the framed lithograph of a woman. A simple gold-painted frame and old wavy glass had captured the intriguing image of a woman from the 1890s. Mike would lie in bed and stare up at the woman with milky white skin, large eyes, a pleasant smile, and lovely, flowing, reddish-brown hair. She stared back at him. The adolescent boy thought this was the most beautiful woman he had ever seen and wondered who she was and why she was hanging there. Fantasizing about her, in his mind he would run his hand over her long hair, touch her cheek softly, and slowly kiss her lips.

When he wasn't at the farm, the young boy was busy building things—a stagecoach, a Civil War cannon and a World War II airplane with British markings in which he pulled his little brother around. Although no one else in his family was interested in aviation, Mike became passionate about airplanes and was amazed that he could identify them from a distance by their shape and sound. As an adult, the sound of a Merlin engine, used in World War II fighter planes, still brings tears to his eyes. To Mike, it's like listening to music.

He built what seemed like hundreds of model airplanes and studied everything he could get his hands on about aviation. As a Boy Scout, he joined an aviation Explorer post. He even dreamed of meeting a woman pilot. Needless to say, Mike would later get a license to work on aircraft and plans to get his pilot's license.

But aviation wasn't his only interest. Mike's father, a history teacher, took the family on historical outings, to battlefields and forts. His father built the children their own backyard fort, and the neighborhood children were invited to use it as combination battlefield and movie set. All manner of pageants were created here. Mike's father also brought home historical videos to preview for his classes. Mike was mesmerized with the films. Little did he know that he would end up choosing a career in which he educates people through video production and providing vintage historical films.

Another of the passions Mike developed in his youth was music—playing the fiddle and many other string instruments. He has become an accomplished musician. All his life, Mike dreamed of meeting a woman who loved flying and music with as much passion as he did. After a while, Mike began to think that it was just a dream.

Eight years ago, Mike needed a quality 35 mm camera for his business. The salesman at the local photography shop said, "The one you are looking for is at our other store." Walking into the other shop, Mike addressed the woman behind the counter. When their eyes met, there was instant recognition—a deep feeling that they knew everything about each other. As she showed him the camera, their fingers touched, jolting them like a lightning bolt. He told her that he wanted this camera to copy old black-and-white photos of airplanes. That opened the door. She told him that she was a pilot and loved to fly.

At first, Mike couldn't understand Susan's immediate familiarity; he had forgotten the old picture at the farm. When he finally remembered it, he told Susan about the old portrait of the beautiful woman that had hung in his bedroom at his grandparents'.

After that discussion, Mike was compelled to find that painting. Years after Mike's grandfather died, the farmhouse had been remodeled and the beautiful woman had lived in the attic until the farm was sold. Leaning against a maple tree in the front yard of the farmhouse on the day of the sale, she had stared back at Mike again. An antique dealer bought her, along with some other old picture frames. That was the last time Mike saw her. Now, after searching farm sale records, he tracked her down, just prior to her being lost to him forever at an antique sale.

He took the picture to Susan and held it up for her to see. Her eyes became wide with disbelief. She felt as if she was looking at a mirror of herself! Susan has a fair complexion, lovely smile, and long flowing auburn hair.

The friendship grew. Finally, Mike felt driven to tell Susan about his deep feelings for her. Impulsively, he drove across several states to track her down at a convention. With 100,000 conferees present, it was "synchronistic" that Mike even found her.

By the time he found her, he was grungy from sleeping in his van, and his feet were hurting from spending days walking around the convention.

She arranged for him to come to her friend's, where she was staying, take a shower, and refresh himself. When she met him at the door, she was wearing a long, flowing dress. Her hair was down and loose, much like the woman in the old picture. Susan told Mike that she had the same profound feelings for him as he professed for her.

Since then, the relationship has blossomed. Mike says that the first time they became physical, it was if they were two magnets that had come together and couldn't let go. They are so attuned that they are constantly in a state of déja vu. Together, they say they live synchronistically.

Mike pinches himself that both he and Susan have related careers in photography and videography. Even better, Susan not only is passionate about flying, but plays the piano exquisitely. When she was twelve, after having taken only a few lessons, her mother took her to audition for another teacher. The teacher told Susan's mother that she had never seen anyone who could play at that level without many years of lessons. The first time Susan played for Mike, he felt paralyzed. A wave of emotion washed over him as if his heart was finally remembering how to feel music.

Both Susan and Mike love Celtic music. The droning sound of the bagpipes gives them goosebumps. Listening to the fiddle moves Susan, as does Irish dancing.

Both Susan and Mike are attracted to the Middle Ages, castles, and Scotland. When Susan's friends got married in a castle, she was preoccupied, absorbed in her surroundings. The setting triggered a nostalgic feeling, as if her blood were stirring, bringing her to the brink of tears. Yet she didn't know why.

She and Mike have felt the same way when they watched the movies *Braveheart* and *Rob Roy*. She also resonated to Marion Zimmer Bradley's *The Mists of Avalon*.

Susan's Celtic-style jewelry is simple with rough, rustic stones. Her favorite clothing designer, Jessica McClintock featured a line called "Gunny Sack" which emphasized long flowing dresses with scoop necks and princess waistlines. She wears linen poet shirts with puffy sleeves and long dresses that lace up the front. This particular dress style, coupled with her long, flowing hair, is a special turn-on for Mike.

In her home, Susan has chosen a simple decor with a mix of earth tones and vibrant colors—dark blues, crimsons, tan. Her furniture is upholstered in rich tapestry. Susan has dreamed of being together with Mike in a stone castle with high walls, wrought iron, and ornate, hand-carved wood furniture. In each case, they were dressed in medieval attire.

When Mike returned from a trip to the Scottish Highlands, Susan got tears in her eyes as she looked at his
photographs. The geography of the Highlands calls to
her, as did the pictures.

With all these past-life clues bombarding them, Mike
decided it was time to have a regression. Under hypnosis, he found himself a bedraggled, hungry, tired wan-
derer. His feet hurt. His hair was matted. As he meandered
through a small medieval Scottish town, a beautiful
young woman with long, flowing hair stood in the door-
way of her cottage.

She smiled and invited him in. She fed him and cared
for him. He got cleaned up and stayed. Forever. In fact,
the love birds rarely left their nest, staying home, sitting
by the fire. Sharing, talking, loving. In later years, Mike
recalls working as a professor. An uneventful life? Mike
prefers to look at it as a soul vacation with his soulmate,
Susan.

I couldn't help but remind Mike of the time he decided
to declare his feelings to Susan and met her in a grimy
state. He says, even now, she feeds him and "gently"
cares for him. These days, Susan jokes about whether she
bakes bread like she used to in their medieval past life.

In fact, after seeing a book on castles, Susan began to
describe in vivid, accurate detail the furniture and the
layout of the room Mike had seen in his Medieval regression. While sharing this, the pair now say they remember this life as if it were yesterday.

Besides this restful lifetime, Mike had another past-
life recall on his own. He found he was from Scotland
and flying for the Royal Air Force during World War II.
What surprised Mike was that he had expected to be
American. Instead, when he looked down at his feet, he
was wearing British flier boots.

He remembers flying in a single-seat British fighter

plane, a Spitfire. Shot down over the English Channel, he struggled with his harness which was wrapped around him. Unable to free himself, he drowned after his plane crashed. Mike, who had previously had a fear of water, said he felt relief after facing and releasing the cause of his unconscious fear.

During his past-life recall, Mike sensed a woman making a trip to the White Chiffs to look over the channel and see physically where he had died. He sensed that he had left this woman before, dying in battle and never returning. On one occasion when Mike dropped Susan off for a class in this life, she remarked mournfully, "Whatever you do, don't leave me." A flood of emotions overcame Mike. He cancelled his plans and didn't leave her.

Mike had another synchronistic happening on his trip to England. He felt "weird" when he toured the operations room for the Battle of Britain. Then he visited the airfield. Overhead, out of nowhere, came a Spitfire. Mike had his own personal air show. When the pilot landed, Mike turned to his friend and said, "I can go home now. Now I know why I came to England."

Being around plane engines with Mike drives Susan crazy. Is it because she remembers how she lost him when he was shot down over the English Channel?

Interestingly, in this life Susan is a pilot. She always wanted to fly from the time she was a little girl and her grandfather took her flying in his plane. Her flight instructor told her, "Sometimes you fly like you've known how for years." Her flight examiner for her private pilot license told her that she has a touch that people who have flown thousands of hours often don't have. Susan says she always flies well when she recalls a book that characterizes a female pilot who ferried planes in World War II, Judith Krantz' *Til We Meet Again.*

Was Susan a pilot herself, or did she "acquire" these

abilities through osmosis from her soulmate?

Regardless, both Susan and Mike say they "were protected by oblivion" until they met each other. Having met their spiritual partners, they have looked for and identified past-life clues which became their wake-up call. They no longer feel that they are sleepwalking through life but are fully awakening to who they are, aided by the knowledge of who they have been.

Now, let's turn our focus to the clues that you have been gathering throughout the book. The first step in the process of interpreting your own clues is to gather them together. Go back and review your answers to the Thought Stimulators at the end of each chapter. Summarize the responses that give you insight into your clues and jot them down under each corresponding section.

COMPILING A BRIEF SUMMARY OF YOUR CLUES:

Clue 1:   A Strong Interest in a Historical Time Period

    1.

    2.

    3.

Clue 2:   Fascination with a Geographical Area or Setting

    1.

    2.

    3.

Clue 3: Art, Artifacts, Music, Dance that Resonates

1.

2.

3.

Clue 4: Your Taste in Fashion, Jewelry, and Home Decor

1.

2.

3.

Clue 5: Books and Movies that Resonate

1.

2.

3.

Clue 6: Vocations, Avocations, Education

1.

2.

3.

Clue 7:   Knowledge or Talent Beyond Experience

1.

2.

3.

Clue 8:   Childhood

1.

2.

3.

Clue 9:   Recurring Patterns

1.

2.

3.

Clue 10: Physical Reactions, Sensations, Emotions

1.

2.

3.

Clue 11: Dreams and Visions

1.

2.

3.

Clue 12: Déja Vu

1.

2.

3.

Clue 13: Strong Feelings about Someone You've Just Met

1.

2.

3.

Clue 14: Preferences and Personalities

1.

2.

3.

Clue 15: Joking about Past Lives

    1.

    2.

    3.

Clue 16: Synchronistic Experiences

    1.

    2.

    3.

BEGINNING THE INTERPRETATION PROCESS OF YOUR PAST-LIFE CLUES

Piecing together your past-life clues is like working on a human jigsaw puzzle. Once you have the pieces on the table and they have taken shape and color, you can move them around and experiment with where they might fit. The more details you have, the more precise you can be in beginning to identify your past lives.

Start with the most obvious details first. After selecting your strongest clues, you can put those pieces in the center of the table, using them as a focal point, anchor, or backdrop. For example:

• Spending one weekend a month recreating another time period such as the American Civil War, the Middles Ages, or World War II

• Wanting to go to Egypt ever since you can remember

• Having an unexplained fear of water or flying

• Getting the creeps while touring the Roman Colosseum.

Next, you can let the other clues go out from that central point like the spokes of a wheel.

Fill in all the clues, even if they appear to be insignificant. As you do this part of the exercise, other clues may be triggered. Leave room for information that might come later.

At this point, you may have to make some assumptions or use your right brain to imagine a little; e.g.,:

• Having a fascination for twelfth-century Scotland and liking woodworking could indicate a lifetime as a carpenter in Scotland.

• Designing and sewing medieval outfits as a child could be evidence of a life as a medieval seamstress.

• Making a World War II British airplane as a child might mean a lifetime as a pilot or mechanic during that war.

• Having a deathly fear of black boots, barbed wire and European sirens could signify a lifetime in a Nazi concentration camp.

Now, you may begin to see the big picture. You may be able to observe interconnections, patterns, and relationships. Reviewing Nora's Charlottesville journey can refresh your understanding of making interpretations and correlations.

If you are interested in exploring details as to how and where you knew another person in a past life, you can record that information as well. Look for clues you have in common. Are you drawn to the same time period? Do you have issues in common?

Having information related to other lifetimes, you can chart each past life individually so that you can more fully explore them.

INSTRUCTIONS FOR CHART 1:
YOUR PAST-LIFE SKETCH

Before completing this, you may want to refer to Nora's past-life sketch (chart 4) in the Appendix.

1. Fill in the larger circles first.
2. Work with clusters when possible and make interconnections.
3. Don't worry if there are empty spaces.
4. Review your past-life sketch.
5. Summarize your clues and record: "Findings" that could indicate a type of past-life person, lifestyle, or lifetime you found; related "Issues" that have come to your attention; and "Attitude Changes" that would be advantageous as a result of your understanding of this past lifetime.
6. Review your chart periodically to see if you can fill in more details.
7. When you feel satisfied that you have uncovered the bulk of the clues about one lifetime, become aware of clues to another past life. Work with a new chart.

There are additional past-life sketches for other lifetimes. Sections on lifetime overviews and combined past-life sketches are located in the Appendix.

Chart 1
Past-Life
Sketch
Life 1

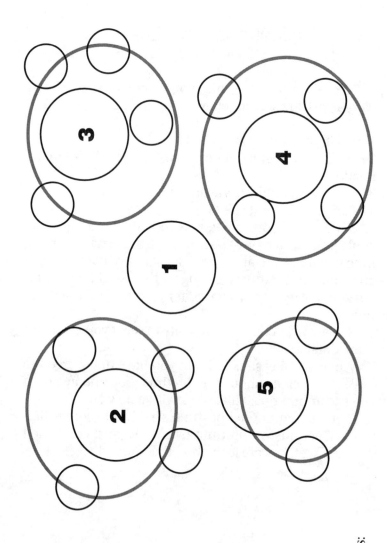

Findings:

Issues:

Attitude Changes:

Chart 1
Past-Life
Sketch
Life 2

1

2

3

4

5

Findings:

Issues:

Attitude Changes:

Chart 1
Past-Life
Sketch
Life 3

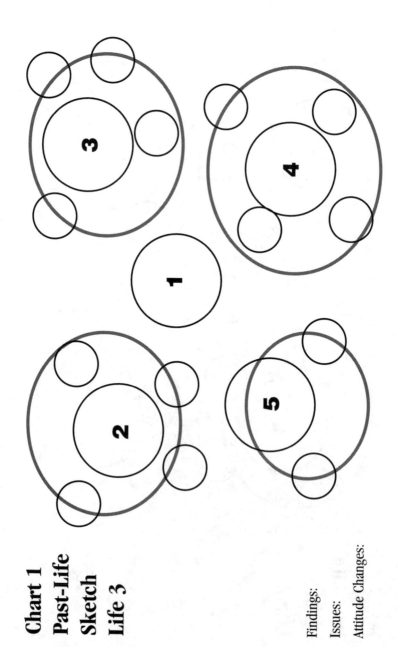

Findings:

Issues:

Attitude Changes:

CHART 2: AN OVERVIEW OF YOUR LIFETIMES

Transfer your reviewed and recorded past-life information here.

LIFE REVIEW #1

Findings:

Issues:

Attitude Changes:

Relates to current life:

LIFE REVIEW #2

Findings:

Issues:

Attitude Changes:

Relates to current life:

LIFE REVIEW #3

Findings:

Issues:

Attitude Changes:

Relates to current life:

Chart 3: An Overview of Your Lifetimes

Record the previous summary, similarities, and differences between lifetimes. Look for life patterns and insights that emerge.

Life	Summary	Similarities	Differences	Patterns
1	F I A R			
2	F I A R			
3	F I A R			

F = FINDINGS

I = ISSUES

A = ATTITUDES

R = RELATES

A STEP-BY-STEP PROCESS FOR APPLYING THESE CLUES TO YOUR PAST LIVES.

Step 1   *Record the clues* that you have found through self-discovery, meditation, dreams, or synchronicity. Ask friends what clues they observe in you.

Step 2.   *Piece together clues.* Begin to observe patterns that relate to your present life. Match your clues with those of other significant people in your life. Add new clues as they are revealed.

Step 3.   *Address past-life issues* that arise. Ask your guides or higher self the lessons for which this past-life was designed and its impact on your current life. Don't judge your past actions. Forgive yourself and others in that life.

Step 4.   *Reframe unempowering past-life scenes.* In a relaxed, meditative state, replay any past-life scenes in which you preferred a positive outcome. Rewrite the script and imagine playing an empowered role or correcting a character flaw or pattern.

Step 5.   *Choose to make changes* in attitude and action by replacing past unproductive patterns with healthy ones. Create an affirmation or positive "I am" statement about the new life-enhancing patterns in your life. Visualize those changes now.

Step 6.   *Validate past-life information* by monitoring whether it resonates and feels comfortable over time. If you ask your higher self for validation, it will come through dreams, meditation, or synchronistic experiences.

Step 7. *Explore another lifetime* when you have exhausted clues concerning one lifetime. Ask your higher self for information, insights, and a deeper understanding of a particular issue or relationship. Review the Thought Stimulators. Record new insights, hunches, and clues. Refer periodically to your new Past-Life Sketch. Remember, this search is an ongoing one. Enjoy the adventure and the self-discovery.

As you sort out your own clues, you need to be reflective as well as practical.

Have you just exchanged togas and armor for jeans and suits? Sandals for running shoes? Papyrus for laptops? Drumbeats for cellular phones?

Are you making the best of your journey through time?

How much has your life really changed and how much have you, as a person, really learned? Wars still rage around us and children are still abused. People can still be unkind, whether in a kindergarten sandbox or a senior citizen's card game. Everyone wants this to be a kinder and gentler world, less brutal than the past; are you applying your lessons?

As you do this self-discovery work, you can make great strides forward, choosing to break—once and for all time—your individual and collective repeated roles that have kept you in bondage to the baser instincts through the centuries.

I am convinced that if you are willing to explore your past-life clues, let them fall into place, allow yourself to see your current life and relationships from a fresh perspective, and make the warranted life-enhancing changes, you will be more at peace with your world and yourself.

You may find that you will attract more of what you want in your life as you unravel the past and free yourself from what no longer serves you. You will begin to find you are no longer a victim but are more empowered to let go of destructive behaviors, traits, and relationships, and to replace them with life-affirming ones.

As you travel through your past lives, you should remember to be nonjudgmental and forgiving of yourself and others, understanding that the whole picture has not been revealed to you and may never be in this life. You can feel safe, knowing that your subconscious mind will let you see only that for which you are ready.

Although putting your puzzle pieces together may take some time, unfoldment is an evolutionary process—you will find that this is a fascinating journey in self-discovery. Through this deceptively simple process, you can not only create and enjoy more quality in your life, but you may also get a glimpse of your immortal soul.

We are all works in progress, and you need to realize that your quest for soul growth is an ongoing one. Realize that each time you focus on your clues to your past lives, you travel into the sacred time of the soul.

So, keep your seatbelt fastened. Continue to enjoy the process and your adventuresome travel into your past so that your present and future can be filled with peace, joy, and understanding.

Identifying and integrating past-life clues can be your wake-up call. You may no longer feel that you are sleepwalking through life but are fully awakening to who you are, aided by the knowledge of who you have been. You may never look at yourself, your life, or your relationships the same way again.

FOR FURTHER EXPLORATION INTO PAST LIVES

Having individual past-life regression sessions by a trained regression therapist can enhance your own past-life knowledge. Past-life clues that you have already identified should help to fertilize the subconscious mind so that you can more readily consciously retrieve additional information.

Listening to a past-life regression tape can also help you facilitate your personal past-life journey. This can build on and support the material you have received from examining your past-life clues. After regression sessions, you should continue to observe clues, whether internal or external, that may be subtle or become increasingly apparent in your life.

To find a reputable regression therapist in your area, contact the Association for Past-Life Research and Therapies (APRT), P.O. Box 20151, Riverside, CA 92516, at 909-784-1570.

Copies of my regression audio tape, "Experience a Past Life: A Guided Journey" are available from the A.R.E. Press, 1-800-723-1112.

❖

Appendix

Chart 4
Nora:
Past-Life

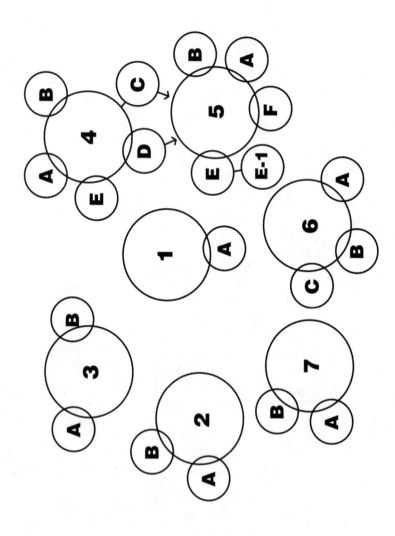

Findings:

Issues:

Attitude Changes:

FREE *CATALOG OF BOOKS* AND *MEMBERSHIP ACTIVITIES*

Fill-in and mail this postage-paid card today.

Please write clearly

Name: _____

Address: _____

City: _____

State/Province: _____

Postal/Zip Code: _____ Country: _____

421-6
4/99

Association for Research and Enlightenment, Inc.
215 67th Street
Virginia Beach, VA 23451-2061

For Faster Service call 1-800-723-1112
www.are-cayce.com

KEY TO CHART 4: NORA'S PAST-LIFE SKETCH

1. Message: "Go Chalotsvile"

   A. Child (of Thomas Jefferson: TJ)

2. Uncle Fred-TJ scholar

   A. Nora's anger at TJ (as child)

   B. Fred raises $ to buy Monticello

3. Reads Hemings book

   A. Authored by friend

   B. Gut feeling—son Beverly Hemings

4. House sale when shopping

   A. Visits Monticello at age 20

   B. Charlottesville meets relocation criteria

   C. Never visits Monticello after move

   D. Anger at TJ, slavery

   E. Originally TJ's property

5. Nora's caretaker

   A. Psychic foretold Nora's arrival

   B. "I'm home"

   C. Never visits Monticello

   D. Anger at TJ, slavery

   E. Regression as Peter, TJ's cook

1.   A cook now

F. Wife-Critta, a Hemings

6. Nora recognizes Polly Jefferson

A. "Polly" recalls scenes as a Jefferson

B. Husband Meriwether Lewis

C. Nora's friend

7. Astrology Reading

A. Son of chief

B. Slave

FINDINGS: Beverly Hemings, fifth child of Jefferson and Sally Hemings

ISSUES: Anger at Jefferson and slavery issue

ATTITUDE CHANGES: Developing compassion and peace

Chart 5
Combined
Past-Life
Sketch

CLUES IN COMMON

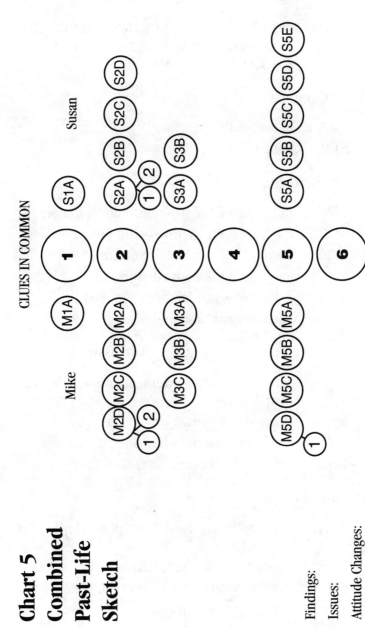

Mike   Susan

Findings:

Issues:

Attitude Changes:

KEY TO CHART 5: MIKE AND SUSAN'S COMBINED
PAST-LIFE SKETCH
CLUES-IN-COMMON

1. Painting

    M1A: In love with
    S1A: Look alike

2. Love of flying

    M2A: Kid: Built WWII airplanes, models, scouts
    M2B: Engines: identify, love, work on
    M2C: Trip to England: WW II Spitfire
    M2D: Past life as pilot who drowns
             1. Fear of water lessens
             2. Leaves woman behind
    S2A: Pilot
             1. Exceptional abilities
             2. Improves after reading about female pilot
                in WW II
    S2B: Wanted to fly since kid
    S2C: Crazy about Mike when around engines
    S2D: Fear of him leaving (see M2D-2)

3. Love of Music

    M3A: Accomplished musician—plays fiddle and
             other strings
    M3B: Loves bagpipes, Scottish music
    M3C: "Struck" when heard Susan play piano
    S3A: Unusual talents in piano

S3B: Loves bagpipes, fiddles, and Celtic music

4. Love at first sight—both

5. Interest in Medieval time period

M5A: Medieval books, movies, music

M5B: Wild about Susan in medieval dress

M5C: Trip to Scotland

M5D: Past-life regression in Scotland with Susan

l. Shower episode similarities

S5A: Loves medieval books, movies, music

S5B: Chooses medieval decor, fashion, jewelry, likes architecture

S5C: Dreams of medieval lifetimes with Mike

S5D: Deja vu at castle

S5E: Jokes about baking bread in medieval life

6. Déja vu and synchronicity—both: frequently

FINDINGS: Together in World War II and Medieval times

ISSUES: Fear of abandonment; fear of water

ATTITUDE CHANGES: Understand why fear of abandonment and water

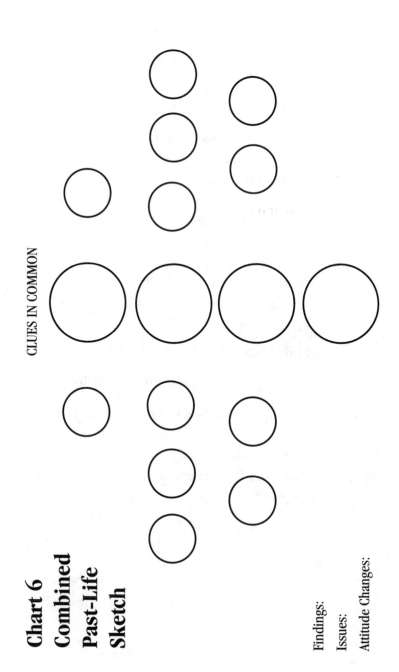

**Chart 6
Combined
Past-Life
Sketch**

CLUES IN COMMON

Findings:

Issues:

Attitude Changes:

CHART 6: A COMBINED PAST-LIFE SKETCH

1. Fill in the Clues-in-Common first.

2. Work with each common clue cluster and make interconnections.

3. Draw lines to connect circles.

4. Don't worry if there are empty spaces.

5. Check back periodically to see if more details unfold.

6. Analyze your Findings, Issues-in-Common, and Attitude Changes.

7. Use both left and right brain to figure out your Issues and Attitude Changes.

Notes

Throughout this book, references have been made to both Civil War and medieval reenactor stories, some of which have been excerpted from the author's two prior books. For more information, see:

Echoes from the Battlefield: First-Person Accounts of Civil War Past Lives by Barbara Lane. 1996.
Echoes from Medieval Halls: Past-Life Memories from the Middle Ages by Barbara Lane. 1997.
Both were published by the A.R.E. Press, 1-800-723-1112.

Chapter 3

1. *Many Mansions*, Gina Cerminara, p. 184.

Chapter 5

1. "Gamesmanship" in *People Weekly* by Chuck Arnold, p. 162.

Chapter 6

1. *Edgar Cayce on Reincarnation*, Noel Langely, p. 84.
2. *Leading with My Chin: Jay Leno*, Jay Leno with Bill Zehme.
3. *You Have Been Here Before*, Edith Fiore, PH.D. p. 8.

Chapter 7

1. *Children Who Remember Previous Lives: A Question of Reincarnation*, Ian Stevenson, M.D., p. 180.
2. *Many Mansions*, Gina Cerminara, p. 89.
3. *Child Star: An Autobiography*, Shirley Temple Black.
4. *Many Mansions*, Gina Cerminara, p. 89.

Chapter 8

1. *My Sister Marilyn: A Memoir of Marilyn Monroe*, Berniece Baker Miracle and Mona Rae Miracle.
2. *If I Can Dream: Elvis' Own Story*, Larry Geller and Joel Spector with Patricia Romanowski, pp. 39-40.
3. *Whoopi Goldberg: Her Journey from Poverty to Megastardom*, James Robert Parish.
4. *Grace (Kelly) of Monaco: An Interpretive Biography*, Steven Englund.
5. *Gracie: A Love Story*, George Burns.
6. *Misha: The Mikhail Baryshnikov Story*, Barbara Aria.
7. *Bach*, Eva Mary and Sydney Grew.
8. *Children Who Remember Previous Lives: A Question of Reincarnation*, Ian Stevenson, M.D., p. 180.
9. *Past Lives, Future Lives*, Dr. Bruce Goldberg, p. 269.
10. *Children Who Remember Previous Lives: A Question of Reincarnation, op. cit.*, p. 182.
11. *Children's Past Lives: How Past-Life Memories Affect Your Child*, Carol Bowman, p. 172.

Chapter 9

1. "Princess Tells of Pain, Depression, Romance, and the Palace Enemy," BBC interview with Martin Bashir in *Princess Diana: Her Life in Words and Pictures*, September 1997, pp. 62-65.
2. Edgar Cayce life reading 5753-2.

Other sources for Princess Diana include:
"Who's to Blame for Diana's Death?" Gregg Easterbrook, *U.S. News & World Report*, September 15, 1997, pp. 22-26.
"Diana: Princess of Wales," *People Tribute: Special Collector's Issue*, Fall 1997.
"Tribute to Princess Diana," *Time Commemorative Issue*, September 15, 1997.

Chapter 10

1. *Woody Allen: A Biography,* Eric Lax.
2. *You Have Been Here Before,* Edith Fiore, Ph.D., p. 6.
3. *Beyond the Ashes,* Rabbi Yonassan Gershom, pp. 128-152.
4. *Ibid.*
5. "The Evidence for Survival from Claimed Memories of Former Incarnations, Part I: Review of the Data;" "Part 2: Analysis of the Data and Suggestions for Further Investigations," *Journal of the American Society for Psychical Research,* Ian Stevenson, M.D., April and October 1960.
6. *Reliving Past Lives: The Evidence Under Hypnosis,* Helen Wambach.
7. *Coming Back,* Raymond Moody.

Chapter 11

1. *Lifetimes: True Accounts of Reincarnation,* Frederick Lenz.
2. *The Search for Yesterday: A Critical Examination of the Evidence of Reincarnation,* Scott D. Rogo.
3. *Life Beyond Life: The Evidence for Reincarnation,* Hanz Holzer.
4. *Living Your Past Lives,* Karl Schlotterbeck.

Chapter 13

1. "Warren Gamaliel Harding," George E. Mowry, *Collier's Encyclopedia,* 1997 edition.
2. "Citizens of Harding's Hometown Compare Presidential Dalliances," Mary Otto, *Knight-Ridder/Tribune News Service,* August 24, 1998.
3. *Presidential Sex,* Wesley O. Hagood, p. 91.
4. *Ibid.* p. 90.
5. "Citizens of Harding's Hometown Compare Presidential Dalliances," *op. cit.*
6. *Presidential Sex, op. cit.,* p. 96.
7. *The Strange Death of President Harding,* Gaston B. Means

with May Dixon Thacker.

8. *Presidential Sex, op. cit.*, p. 99.
9. *The Strange Death of President Harding, op. cit.*
10. *Ibid.*
11. *The Wives of Henry VIII*, Antonio Fraser.
12. *Ibid.*
13. *The Six Wives of Henry VIII*, Alison Weir.
14. *The Wives of Henry VIII, op. cit.*
15. *Ibid.*
16. *The Six Wives of Henry VIII, op. cit.*

Chapter 14

1. "Daring to Go There," Ron Stodghill, *Time*, October 5, 1998, p. 81.
2. "Oprah's Moment," Jonathan Van Meter, *Vogue*, October, 1998, p. 328.
3. "Oprah's Summer Dream," Oprah Winfrey, *Time*, October 5, 1998, p. 79.
4. "Oprah's Moment," *op. cit.*, p. 329.
5. *Edgar Cayce on Reincarnation*, Noel Langley, p. 84.
6. *Many Lifetimes*, Denys Kelsey and Joan Grant, p. 21.

Other sources on Oprah Winfrey:
    "Oprah: 'These Are the Glory Days for Me,'" Ann Oldenburg, *USA Today*, October 8, 1998, pp. D1-2.
    "No Peace from a Brutal Legacy," Janet Maslin, *New York Times*, October 16, 1998, pp. E-1, E-20.

Chapter 15

1. *Gracie: A Love Story*, George Burns.
2. *Past-Lives Therapy*, Morris Netherton and Nancy Shiffrin.
3. *101 Ways to Avoid Reincarnation: Or Getting It Right the*

First Time, Hester Mundis, p. 69.

4. *Reincarnation: Claiming Your Past, Creating Your Future,* Lynn Elwell Sparrow, p. 45.

Chapter 16

1. *If I Can Dream: Elvis' Own Story,* Larry Geller and Joel Spector with Patricia Romanowski, pp. 30-37.

2. *Ibid.*

3. *Elizabeth Taylor: A Celebration,* Sheredan Morley.

4. *Journey of Souls: Case Studies of Life Between Lives,* Michael Newton, Ph.D., pp. 260-261.

Bibliography

"American Spectacle, An" *Newsweek* (October 16, 1995).

Aria, Barbara. *Misha: The Mikhail Baryshnikov Story.* New York, N.Y.: St. Martin's Press, 1989.

Arnold, Chuck. "Gamesmanship" in *People Weekly* (October 20, 1997, Vol. 48, No. 16), p. 162.

Bashir, Martin (BBC interview). "Princess Tells of Pain, Depression, Romance, and the Palace Enemy," in *Princess Diana: Her Life in Words and Pictures* (September 1997), pp. 62-65.

Black, Shirley Temple. *Child Star: An Autobiography.* New York, N.Y.: McGraw-Hill Pub. Co., 1988.

Bowman, Carol. *Children's Past Lives: How Past-Life Memories Affect Your Child.* New York: N.Y.: Bantam Books, 1997.

Bucky, Peter A. *The Private Albert Einstein.* Kansas City: Andrews & McMeal, 1993.

Burns, George. *Gracie: A Love Story.* New York, N.Y.: G.P. Putnam's Sons, 1988.

Callan, Michael Feeney. *Sean Connery.* Briarcliff, N.Y.: Stein and Day, Pub., 1983.

Cerminara, Gina. *Many Mansions.* New York, N.Y.: Sloane, 1970.

"Diana: Princess of Wales," *People Tribute: Special Collector's Issue* (Fall 1997).

Easterbrook, Gregg. "Who's to Blame for Diana's Death?" *U.S. News & World Report* (September 15, 1997), pp. 22-26.

Englund, Steven. *Grace (Kelly) of Monaco: An Interpretive Biography*. Garden City, N.Y.: Doubleday & Co., Inc., 1984.

Fiore, Edith, Ph.D. *You Have Been Here Before*. New York, N.Y.: Ballantine Books, 1978.

Francis, Wayne. "Another Swimsuit." *News Group Newspapers, Ltd.* (January 4, 1993).

Fraser, Antonia. *The Wives of Henry VIII*. New York, N.Y.: Alfred A. Knopf, 1992.

Geller, Larry; Spector, Joel; with Patricia Romanowski. *If I Can Dream: Elvis' Own Story*. New York, N.Y.: Simon & Schuster, 1989.

Gershom, Rabbi Yonassan. *Beyond the Ashes*. Virginia Beach, Va.: A.R.E. Press, 1992.

——— *From Ashes to Healing*. Virginia Beach, Va.: A.R.E. Press, 1996.

Goldberg, Bruce, Dr. *Past Lives, Future Lives*. New York, N.Y.: Ballantine Books, 1982.

Grew, Eva Mary and Sydney. *Bach*. New York, N.Y.: Collier Books, 1962.

Hagood, Wesley O. *Presidential Sex*. New York, N.Y.: Carol Pub. Group, 1995.

Holzer, Hanz. *Life Beyond Life: The Evidence for Reincarnation*. West Nyack, N.Y.: Parker, 1985.

Iacocco, Lee. *Iacocco: An Autobiography*. New York, N.Y.: Bantam Books, 1986.

Kelsey, Denys, and Grant, Joan. *Many Lifetimes.* London, England: Corgi, 1976.

Lane, Barbara. *Echoes from the Battlefield: First-Person Accounts of Civil War Past Lives.* Virginia Beach, Va.: A.R.E. Press, 1996.

———— *Echoes from Medieval Halls: Past-Life Memories from the Middle Ages.* Virginia Beach, Va.: A.R.E. Press, 1997.

Langely, Noel. *Edgar Cayce on Reincarnation.* London, England: Howard Baker, 1969.

Lax, Eric. *Woody Allen: A Biography.* New York, N.Y.: Alfred Knopf, 1991.

Leno, Jay, with Bill Zehme. *Leading with My Chin: Jay Leno.* New York, N.Y.: HarperCollins, 1996.

Lenz, Frederick. *Lifetimes: True Accounts of Reincarnation.* New York, N.Y.: Ballantine Books, 1986.

Lucas, Winafred Blake, Ph.D. *Regression Therapy: A Handbook for Professionals.* Visalia, Cal.: Deep Forest Press, Vol. 1, p. 83.

Maslin, Janet. "No Peace from a Brutal Legacy," *New York Times* (October 16, 1998), E-1, E-20.

Means, Gaston B., with May Dixon Thacker. *The Strange Death of President Harding.* New York, N.Y.: Guild Publishing Corp., 1930.

Miracle, Berniece Baker, and Mona Rae. *My Sister Marilyn: A Memoir of Marilyn Monroe.* Chapel Hill, N.C.: Algonquin Books, 1994.

Moody, Raymond. *Coming Back.* New York, N.Y.: Bantam, 1991.

Morley, Sheredan. *Elizabeth Taylor: A Celebration.* Great Britain: Butler & Tanner, Ltd., 1982.

Mowry, George E. "Warren Gamaliel Harding," *Collier's Encyclopedia* (1997 edition).

Mundis, Hester. *101 Ways to Avoid Reincarnation: Or Getting It Right the First Time.* New York, N.Y.: Workman Pub., 1969.

Netherton, Morris, and Shiffrin, Nancy. *Past-Lives Therapy.* New York, N.Y.: Morrow, 1978.

Newton, Michael, Ph.D. *Journey of Souls: Case Studies of Life Between Lives.* St. Paul, Minn.: Llewellyn Pub., 1996.

Oldenburg, Ann. "Oprah: 'These Are the Glory Days for Me,'" *USA Today* (October 8, 1998), D1-2.

Otto, Mary. "Citizens of Harding's Hometown Compare Presidential Dalliances," *Knight-Ridder/Tribune News Service* (August 24, 1998).

Parish, James Robert. *Whoopi Goldberg: Her Journey from Poverty to Megastardom.* Secaucus, N.J.: Carol Pub. Co., 1997.

Rogo, Scott D. *The Search for Yesterday: A Critical Examination of the Evidence of Reincarnation.* EnglewoodCliffs, N.J.: Prentice Hall, 1985.

Schlotterbeck, Karl. *Living Your Past Lives: The Psychology of Past-Life Regression.* New York, N.Y.: Ballantine Books, 1987.

Sparrow, Lynn Elwell. *Reincarnation: Claiming Your Past, Creating Your Future.* New York, N.Y.: St. Martin's Paperbacks, 1988.

Stevenson, Ian, M.D. *Children Who Remember Previous Lives:*

A Question of Reincarnation. Charlottesville, Va.: University Press of Virginia, 1997.

——— "The Evidence for Survival from Claimed Memories of Former Incarnations, Part I: Review of the Data." "Part 2: Analysis of the Data and Suggestions for Further Investigations," *Journal of the American Society for Psychical Research,* (Vol. 54, April and October 1960).

Steyn, Mark. "James Stewart's Fear of Flying" in *National Review* (August 11, 1997), Vol. 49, No. 15, p. 48.

Stodghill, Ron. "Daring to Go There," *Time* (October 5, 1998), p. 81.

Sun Times (London, May 5, 1974).

Teichmann, Howard. *Fonda: My Life as Told to Howard Teichmann.* New York: N.Y.: New American Library, 1981.

"Tribute to Princess Diana," *Time Commemorative Issue* (September 15, 1997).

Van Meter, Jonathan. "Oprah's Moment," *Vogue* (October 1998), p. 328.

Wambach, Helen, Ph.D. *Reliving Past Lives: The Evidence Under Hypnosis.* New York, N.Y.: Harper & Row, 1978.

Weir, Alison. *The Six Wives of Henry VIII.* New York, N.Y.: Grove Weidenfeld, 1991.

Winfrey, Oprah. "Oprah's Summer Dream," *Time* (October 5, 1998), p. 79.

Woolger, Roger, Ph.D. *Other Lives, Other Selves: A Jungian Psychologist Discovers Past Lives.* New York, N.Y.: Bantam Books, 1987.

About the Author

Barbara Lane, Ph.D., is a clinical hypnotherapist in private practice, who was trained by some of the foremost regression therapists She is a member of the Association for Past-Life Research and Therapies and a certified Reiki master who combines alternative and traditional healing in her practice.

Ms. Lane is the author of two books based on her experiences in regressing historical reenactors to past lives: *Echoes from the Battlefield: First-Person Accounts of Civil War Past Lives* and Echoes *from Medieval Halls: Past-Life Memories from the Middle Ages.* She also addressed Civil War reenactors and conducted group regressions at the 135th observance of the Battle of Gettysburg.

Ms. Lane holds several degrees, including a Ph.D. in metapsychology and an M.A. in metaphysics from Westbrook University, New Mexico, as well as a B.A. in history from Mercy College, Michigan.

Since the publication of her books, Ms. Lane has become a popular guest on radio and television, including news and feature programs in Boston, Phoenix, Chicago, and Washington, D.C. She also was a guest on the Howard Stern show, during which she regressed several of his staff members on the air. She also has been featured on the *Sightings* TV program and in newspapers around the country, including the *Washington Post*, the

Philadelphia Inquirer, the *Village Voice,* and many others.

The Michigan native not only has worked as a reporter, anchor, producer, and director in radio and television, but she is developing plans to host a syndicated television show on past-life regression. In addition, she has worked as a crisis counselor and case manager for a homeless shelter. She currently lives and works in Alexandria, Virginia.

For information on regression workshops, speaking engagements or private sessions, Ms. Lane can be contacted at:

P.O. Box 25502
Alexandria, VA 22313.

Or via e-mail at Echoes11@aol.com (please understand if a reply takes some time). Readers also can visit her Web site at http://members.aol.com/echoes11/barbara.htm.

A.R.E. PRESS

The A.R.E. Press publishes quality books, videos, and audiotapes meant to improve the quality of our readers' lives—personally, professionally, and spiritually. We hope our products support your endeavors to realize your career potential, to enhance your relationships, to improve your health, and to encourage you to make the changes necessary to live a loving, joyful, and fulfilling life.

For more information or to receive a free catalog, call:

1-800-723-1112

Or write:

A.R.E. Press
215 67th Street
Virginia Beach, VA 23451-2061